LIVING JUSTICE

REVOLUTIONARY COMPASSION IN A BROKEN WORLD

JAMIE GATES AND JON MIDDENDORF

{UNDERCURRENT SERIES}

Barefoot Ministries®

Kansas City, Missouri

Copyright 2007
by Barefoot Ministries®

ISBN 978-0-8341-5019-5

Printed in the United States of America

Editor: Bo Cassell
Assistant Editor: Stephanie McNelly
Cover Design: Lindsey Rohner
Interior Design: Sharon R. Page

Library of Congress Cataloging-in-Publication Data

Gates, Jamie, 1971-
    Living justice : revolutionary compassion in a broken world / by Jamie Gates and Jon Middendof.
        p. cm. — (Undercurrent series)
    ISBN 978-0-8341-5019-5
    1. Social justice—Religious aspects—Christianity. 2. Christianity and justice. 3. Christian sociology. 4. Compassion—Religious aspects—Christianity. 5. Youth—Religious life. I. Middendorf, Jon. II. Title.
    BT738.G34 2007
    261.8—dc22

                                                                                    2007020051

10 9 8 7 6 5 4 3 2 1

Jon would like to dedicate this book to

- my wife, Kelly, and our two kids, Taylor and Drew, who support my ministry by loving me,
- the ministry team at OKC First Church of the Nazarene, led by Dr. Steve Green, who have fanned the flame in me, and
- to my parents, Jesse and Susan, who have faithfully embodied the gospel from the very first.

Jamie would like to dedicate this book to

- Charisa, my firstborn, whose wisdom and musical gifts inspire me,
- Anthony, whose energy and sensitivity humble me,
- Micaela, whose joy and wonder reminds me of the mystery of God, and
- Michelle, whose love and faithfulness speaks sacramental grace to me daily.

Jon Middendorf is the proud husband of Kelly and the proud father of Taylor and Drew. He continues to be deeply committed to the family of faith at OKC First Nazarene, where he has pastored and served since 1990. In addition, Jon serves as the consultant for NYI (Nazarene Youth International) for Big Picture Training, a ministry designed to equip and encourage volunteer youth ministers.

Jamie Gates serves as associate professor of cultural anthropology in the Department of Sociology and Social Work and as the Director of the Center for Justice and Reconciliation at Point Loma Nazarene University. Raised in South Africa during the difficult Apartheid years, Jamie studies and works toward justice and reconciliation as core theological and social concerns.

CONTENTS

CHAPTER 1
INTRODUCTION–
LEAVING OUT
LEFT BEHIND

Picture this: two students are driving home from different church gatherings on a Sunday afternoon. They attend different churches, but they live in the same large and growing city, in the same part of town. The drive home takes each by the same ugly city scenes, and while they notice the scars and effects of crime and poverty in the faces of their fellow city-citizens, their reactions to what they see are completely different.

TIM'S VIEW

Our first student, Tim, sees the pain and devastation as evidence that the world is in fact going to hell at cable-internet speeds. With every news story about the next violent crime, with every new letter of graffiti, with every rumor of local and global unrest, Tim sees the fracture of the world as something that is *supposed* to happen—predicted in Scripture and dramatized in books and movies, not to mention talked about in the never-ending conversations in the church hallways. "The world is falling apart, just like they said it would," Tim mutters to himself as he drives by.

Tim accepts the world as it comes to him—dangerous, violent, and broken. Can you blame him? Sure all the troubles in the world seem too big for one person to fix. More than that,

Tim's belief system is the result of his upbringing. He has been raised in a way that defines "Christianity" as a religion of individuals. It is a meaningful word to Tim, but deeply spiritual and personal. It confronts him at every turn: his thoughts, speech, actions, and attitudes because, if Christianity is living in the way of Jesus, Tim is painfully aware that he falls short all the time. So it is no surprise that Tim has placed the highest priority on his own soul and his own sense of purity.

Make no mistake, Tim is deeply committed. He has worked hard to deny his own broken humanness. He prays, reads Scripture, and attends and supports his church's activities all in the hopes of attaining and maintaining an acceptable level of Christlikeness. Not only that, but Tim is always on the lookout for those who don't yet have a relationship with Christ. He is proud to share his faith and is pretty good at it. He's a good friend who is a good listener, easy to talk to, and great to be around. When given an opportunity, he gives himself in service. He strives for the righteousness he reads about in Scripture—and righteous is where you are measured and found to be without blemish or stain.

If you were to ask Tim to define or describe the term "hope," he would say "hanging in and hanging on" until death or until Jesus comes back and rescues us from this decaying planet and life. His challenge is to stay clean and strong in his faith, distancing himself from all of those influences and influencers who might damage or stain his Christian witness. The broken and evil places in the world are not so much challenges to be overcome as much as they are challenges to Tim's faith and his sense of purity. That being the case, Tim doesn't spend much energy trying to figure out why his city is broken or why people suffer.

In Tim's mind, the world will continue to deteriorate until Christ comes to rescue His people and take them out—to heaven. But in order to keep his place in the next world (whether he gets there in death or by Christ's Second Coming), he must be found pure and blameless when the time is "right." His spirituality is focused on his own salvation. "Justice" on this earth is God's responsibility—it is something that God will do. God will deliver justice to everyone by giving them what they deserve when the end comes.

The result is that Tim sees what is going on around him—and keeps driving.

KARA'S VIEW

Our other student, Kara, sees the same images on her way home. In fact, Kara has seen them for weeks and months, and she too has made a habit of driving past. But this particular day is different.

Kara has grown up in a church and home that define the words "gospel" and "Christianity" more in terms of a "group" than an individual. Faith is as much about the community as it is the individual members. Christianity is not just who she is as an individual believer, but it is something that she and her whole church, and the entire world-wide Church, *practice and embody* for the sake of the planet. The gospel, while she participates in it as an individual, is Good News for all people, anywhere and everywhere, today, no matter their situation or location.

So Kara strives for righteousness, which she understands to be defined as right-relatedness—being in right relationship with God and with people. As she grows toward Christian maturity, Kara tries to understand the call to be pure and blameless. She knows that her personal sense of purity or piety helps her to better relate, understand, protect, and minister to the people around her.

Our first student Tim is genuinely thankful for the resurrection of Jesus, believing that the power of the resurrection saves him from death and judgment. Tim feels he will be lifted out of this world just like the resurrected Jesus. Kara, however, is thankful for both the *Cross* and the Resurrection, believing that in the Cross, Christ has identified himself with a broken world. On the Cross, Jesus is the suffering, broken Christ, who has not shielded himself from pain, but came to live among us and identify with us. Kara sees her life as following this model—she identifies with those who are hurting. She understands the power of the Resurrection too—it can bring healing and salvation to those who are in pain—but there is no separation of the two. And so Kara decides to pull over, get out of her car, and begin a new kind of lifestyle. She stops to ask the name of the homeless lady she has passed dozens of times before.

ON THE JOURNEY

At this point, you're probably thinking, "So, who's right and who's wrong? The 'Tim's' or the 'Kara's'?" Before answering that question, I just want to say that this question is a delicate one; one that has been debated for years and years. People have often argued over circumstances, the definitions of words such as "gospel" and "Christianity," and even faith commitments themselves. So let's ask the question this way: Which of the two do you most identify with, Tim or Kara?

We recognize that there are days when both Tim and Kara pull their cars over to serve. Both of these students are on a journey of discovering how God will use them in the world. Neither of them are completely right, or completely wrong. However, our faith perspective can influence how we approach the topic of justice. If we are at a place in our journey that is focused more on our individual, personal faith and life, it is more difficult to consider how our actions affect the lives of others halfway around the world.

Do we have a faith perspective that hinders us from actively taking part in what God is doing to bring justice to those who need it? This is an important question to consider, but your conclusion at this point is not as important as simply asking the question. This book will be a challenge to you to explore new horizons in God's plan to bring justice to this earth.

CHRISTLIKE JUSTICE

How do we live out justice on earth? It may be helpful to look at passages in the Bible that talk about this idea, beginning with a couple of stories that Jesus told to introduce a godly idea of justice to His disciples. First, read the parable of the Good Samaritan found in Luke 10:25-37. You may know the story, a man is robbed and left for dead, and no one helps him except for a Samaritan. Still, it may be helpful to go back and read it again. When you're finished, ask yourself these questions, "How does Christ describe good faith?" and "Who in this parable gets it right?" Next, read the parable of the sheep and the goats found in Matthew 25:31-46. When you're finished, ask yourself the same questions as before. Notice that in each case, there are those who see a need and do nothing, and there are those who see a need and do something.

LESSONS FROM JEREMIAH

Now I'd like to draw your attention to the Old Testament book of Jeremiah. Jeremiah was a prophet to the southern kingdom of Judah and its capital city Jerusalem. At this time (about 500 B.C.), the kingdom of Judah was living in the shadow of the Babylonian Empire, who eventually attacked and captured the city. According to the people hiding within the city walls, the world was falling apart.

Jeremiah offers several reasons for the demise of the country, but the chief reason has to do with bad faith or bad belief— or as Jeremiah called it, amnesia. The Israelites had forgotten how to be the people of God—serving others, especially those most desperately in need. So God persuades Jeremiah to be His messenger, to show the people where they had gone wrong. Take a few moments to read Jeremiah 1:4-10 right now.

There are a couple of things I want you to notice. First, Jeremiah is young when God calls him; in fact, in verse 6, Jeremiah protests that he is too young to do any good. However, God quickly squashes that argument in verses 7-8. God says to Jeremiah, "Do not be afraid . . . for I am with you and will rescue you" (v. 8). Secondly, God commits himself to Jeremiah and promises to be fully present with him in every struggle. This promise is also true for us today—God will be with us.

Then in verse 10, God says to him, "See, today I appoint you over nations and kingdoms to uproot and tear down, to destroy and overthrow, to build and to plant." In this verse, God calls Jeremiah to challenge the way the planet is organized and to make a complete mess of things. Look at the verbs he uses: uproot, tear down, destroy, and overthrow. In other words, God is calling Jeremiah to wreak havoc, *but* not just for havoc's sake. The verbs God gives Jeremiah also includes "build" and "plant." After making a royal mess of things, Jeremiah is to be God's partner in re-creating creation, so good life can happen again.

So where would you suspect that Jeremiah would go to begin

challenging the people of God? You guessed it. He went to the Temple (which would be the same as going to one of our modern day church buildings). But honestly, what if Jeremiah were still alive and showed up at one of our churches—what would happen? You can read what happened back then in Jeremiah 7:1-11. Take a few moments to read it now.

Imagine what this must have looked like. As people are coming into the Temple, they have to physically work their way around a screaming Jeremiah to get through the doors. What's even worse is the message he gives: "You aren't living right! Don't think you're safe just because you find yourself in this place of worship today!" (vv. 9-10, author's paraphrase). So what would "living right" look like? Take note of verses 5-7. God's dream for His people is that they would act *justly* with one another—treating each other well (we'll talk mare about this later)—and that they'd protect the orphans, widows, and aliens among them. ("Aliens" would be the travelers, visitors, foreigners, or people different from them).

In fact, God's people were unique among the nations in the way they were to live out their faith. Their faith was to be demonstrated in the care they would show for others who were most at risk, most on the margins of life. Belief in God (from ancient Jews to today's Christianity) has always measured itself best by its care. We know our faith is "good faith" not by the care we show for those whom we naturally like and love, but in the quality of the care we show to those not at all like us, or to those most at risk.

It doesn't take much conviction to like, love, and care for your best friend or the most popular and well-liked person, but it takes a deep, covenantal commitment to care for those who are on the edges, the ones who are most in need of rescue. Life doesn't or at least hasn't worked for them, and that's where God calls His people to be—in the midst of their need.

In Jeremiah 7:8, the prophet again slams these "religious" people for their lack of care for each other, which is demonstrated by their deeds—stealing, murdering, committing adultery, worshiping other gods, and so on. Unfortunately, it seems like the people of God have perfected the art of sinning and then sacrificing in order to escape the penalties they deserve.

In response to everything that is going on, God asks, "Has this house, which is called by my name, become a den of robbers in your sight?" (v. 11, NRSV). Rather than being a place of sanctuary, confession, forgiveness, and true repentance, God wonders out loud if His house has become the hangout of robbers and evildoers. It's the same line that Jesus quotes when overturning the tables in the Temple courts, hundreds of years later when again, the people of God were misunderstanding God's intention and His dream for us.[1]

ITS NOT FAIR

It's time we took a closer look at this term justice. Let's start with a phrase most of us have been using for years—"THAT'S NOT FAIR!" It's a great phrase, and we know it well. From the time we are children, we quickly begin to recognize when life is out of balance. If you're anything like me (Jon), I picture kids—my own mostly—using that phrase. My two kids are young and similarly aged. The good news is that they are built-in playmates; the bad news has something to do with sibling rivalry and shouting matches.

When I hear my kids say "it's not fair," I respond pretty typically:

- "Life's not fair."

- "Deal with it."
- "Stop complaining."

Maybe there are more constructive ways of coaxing little complainers to a better place, and maybe the above statements and others like them are necessary and healthy, depending on the situation. But in the process, I hope I'm not doing permanent damage to the notion of fairness.

Now that I've written those statements down, they read like more ugly messages sent by our culture and echoed at times in our churches:

- "Worry about yourself and the rest will take care of itself."
- "Mind your own business."

In other words, *your responsibility stops with your responsibility for yourself.*

By the time we "mature" to this mindset, we've lost the Christian notion that we are responsible for others as much as we are for ourselves. In fact, all of creation is our God given responsibility.[2] By the time we become adults, discussions of fairness and equality often become political in nature; words like "fairness" and "equality" begin to be associated with one political party or point of view. Once these ideas are labeled, they are easier to brush aside—and so we keep them on one side of the political fence.

However, regardless of political views, we all need to protect, preserve, and cultivate the idea of fairness. Why? Because it is the beginning of the conversation about godly justice.

JUSTICE IN THE BIBLE

So what does the Bible mean when it uses the word just or justice? My favorite example is found in Micah 6:8: "He has told you, O mortal, what is good; and what does the Lord require of you but to do justice, and to love kindness, and to walk humbly with your God?" (NRSV).

The word "justice" here represents those actions or that posture that seeks to put things right. In Scripture, when things are right, there is balance, equality, harmony, and peace. In fact, when things are right, you have the picture of God's hopes and dreams for life. The heart of God is all about nurturing, supporting and protecting life—all lives and all of life.[3]

Biblical justice is founded on this idea: God cares just as much for the frail, sick, and poor, as He does for the strong, healthy, and rich. "Only the strong survive!" makes a nice bumper sticker or cheer in the locker room, but it doesn't capture the heart of God. So we can assume that it grieves and frustrates the God of all creation when a portion of that creation is neglected or hurt. Justice means that there is balance and equal attention and love given to those who are powerless, hopeless, hurting, and dying—those who may not be able to care for themselves. They are poor, and God's desire is that they be cared for by others. They should not be neglected, ignored, or mistreated. God loves them dearly and has not forgotten them. To "do justice" means that as God-followers, we hope to emulate God's thirst for justice as well as His frustration over injustice.

CHAPTER 2
TWO GREAT TEMPTATIONS—
CITIZEN AND CONSUMER

Imagine that you are a missionary to a culture where Christianity is outlawed because the government in power believes it be a threat to the stability of the country. You would expect the culture of this country to make it difficult to live out your faith, if not dangerous. Instead of churches, crosses, and other religious symbols, imagine that you are surrounded by political or military symbols and pictures of national rulers—the very images this country uses to demonstrate that loyalty to the government and country are high values. The images show, in very specific terms, where you are to put your faith, hope, and trust—trust in the country, or more specifically, in the ruling party that currently leads and controls the country. Finally, imagine that the national military and the local police are ever-present, making sure that everyone, including you, practices model citizenship.

While Christianity might be outlawed, that doesn't mean that worship is absent. In fact, the symbols of the national "religion" hint at the one who is there to take care of all your needs and is worthy of your worship. Instead of worshiping the God of all Creation, all citizens are encouraged to worship the god of the state. Here, "believers" are well-behaved citizens.

Next, I want you to imagine a completely different country in which the "citizens" are measured only by their net worth: their value is calculated by their possessions, the size of their bank accounts and home(s), and the style of their cars. Imagine that the images on billboards and on the local television stations constantly reinforce this way of life. Their religion is a pursuit of the dream of having more. They trust and rely on earning power—having enough money to buy what they need to make them happy. It's not that Christianity is necessarily outlawed in this place, but the citizens here are so busy chasing down the next dollar, hurrying off to buy, borrow, and accumulate, they don't really have time for Christianity.

"Believers" in this country aren't called citizens; they're called consumers. It's in being a consumer that a person "worships" the gods of this country.

As you may already be aware, our "imaginary" stories are very real in many corners of the world, even our own corners!

FROM IMAGINARY LANDS TO REAL BLINDNESS

We are used to missionaries telling us the stories of working in other cultures whose values are in conflict with Christianity. But is it possible that many Christians in North America (U.S.A. and Canada) have been blind to the conflict and contradictions between Christianity and the culture in our own countries?

Could it be that the habits and structures of our culture have weakened our connectedness to God and one another? Have we been unable to see our own involvement in the flaws of the culture around us—would we know if we had traded Christian values for the values of other "gods"?

We can only hope to see our own blindness if we begin to

take seriously the power and influence of the culture around us. We have to realize that there are "counter-relational" forces (what makes us value ourselves above our relationships to God and others) and that these are constantly at work forming and shaping our passions and habits. The question is, are we able to see if these are profoundly shaping us in un-Christian directions?

In this chapter, we are shining the light on two particular challenges to Christianity: the worship of the nation or country (in which believers are citizens before they are Christians) and the worship of wealth (in which believers are consumers before they are Christians). Either of these may hinder our desire and ability to live out God's justice in the world.

In the spring of 2004, cultural studies professor Karl Martin preached a sermon at a Christian College chapel on Romans 11:33—12:2. (Take a moment now to read this passage from the Bible.) Martin noted that he had been exposed to countless sermons and Bible studies on this passage, and most of them boiled down to the simple message: Don't let the world squeeze you into its mold—which most often meant something like "don't submit to peer pressure."

But in this particular sermon Karl took this passage in a direction much deeper and more profound than is often the case:

Now, in my mid-forties, this passage has come back to me in different but powerful ways. I don't think I have much of a problem with peer pressure these days, but the passage remains significant and addresses two central temptations of my life: The temptation to define myself primarily as a *consumer* rather than primarily as a Christian, and the temptation to define myself primarily as a *citizen* rather than primarily as a Christian.

In this sermon, Karl named as temptations two of the most significant forces at work to redefine our lives. These forces run counter to the life of holiness to which we are called in Christ. The "rulers and authorities" (see Ephesians 6:12) that vie for our attention are money and political power. In this book we will call these the "god of the Marketplace" and the "god of the Homeland."

BOUGHT BY THE GOD OF THE MARKET: BEING A CONSUMER FIRST

A good friend of mine adopted a young boy from Guatemala. She is, of course, quickly becoming aware of how different you see the world when you become a parent. While walking through a local grocery chain recently she was amused by a child pushing a miniature shopping cart next to his mother. It looked exactly like an adult shopping cart, but it was about one-fourth the size. She thought of how someday soon she too would be able to share such times with her son. She also thought of the challenges of raising her son, shaping his habits, and forming his character. However, she was not the only one in the room with an interest in forming and shaping her son. A sign on the little cart read "customer in training."

Some call it materialism; some call it "affluenza;"[4] some call it consumerism or the "culture of consumption." It is a pervasive way of thinking in North America. Consumer culture shapes all that we do. The influence of this mindset forms us in many ways that are contradictory to Christ's call and to a life of simplicity and holiness. Consumerism has distracted us from serious involvement in our world—and it may have helped create a larger separation between the rich and the poor. In other words, consumerism has prevented justice.

THE MAKING OF THE NORTH AMERICAN CONSUMER

We can't understand the scope of our buy-in to the culture of consumption without understanding how we got here. It started with Christians being good people—they were hard working and saved their money. At that time, Christians influenced the culture around them (instead of the other way around) and the whole society followed these values.[5] It is no surprise that Christians and those with the same work values were quick to accumulate more than what they needed for their own use. Such a surplus and accumulation of wealth was the beginning of turning us into a culture of consumers.

But even when these economic forces began, people did not immediately change their lifestyle to become consumer minded. Back in 18th-century Great Britain, France, and elsewhere, merchants were concerned that more goods were being produced than could be sold. Nineteenth-century American workers were encouraged to be frugal and save their earnings. Spending, particularly on luxuries, was considered wasteful.

In the early 20th-century there was a major shift in the way we viewed the meaning of goods. This happened in large part due to the way in which goods were presented and displayed. In the 19th-century most products were displayed in bulk with little concern for arrangement. In the 1870s, Ivory Soap and Quaker Oats were the first to display prepackaged items with company labels.[6] In the 1890s, department stores emerged in the United States as major retail establishments and paved the way for shaping the way we think about products. "The department store became a cultural primer telling people how they should dress, furnish their homes, and spend their leisure time."[7] Now catch this—we went from buying bulk goods because we needed them to survive, to stores displaying what we should look like and how we should live.

Three other developments in the early 20th-century warrant mention as key components in making the American consumer: **fashion**, **customer service**, and **consumer credit**. Fashion is the stirring up of anxiety and restlessness over the possession of things that were not new or up-to-date. Fashion pressures us to buy not out of need but for style—from a desire to conform to what someone else defines as fashionable. There is a multi-billion dollar global advertising industry dedicated to creating ever-changing standards for what is in style.

Interest in customer service rose as an attempt to add a human face to what was constructed as an essentially economic transaction. Company executives soon learned that their customers were willing to spend more time and money in their stores if they felt more of a personal connection with the store and its products. Service became part of companies' operating expenses as they found that fawning over customers increased profits.

The final touches on the production of the consumer were made with the creation of consumer credit. We can now borrow what we don't have and bank on the future to pay for the new things and services we supposedly really need now. In other words, credit cards have given us the power to purchase all of the things that are dangled in front of us—without having to decide if we need them or can afford them. It is the perfect fit in an advertising driven culture. First the advertisers create the desire in you to buy a product, and fashion supports this by making you feel left out if you don't. Then the credit card companies help you get it now without having to wait until you actually have the money.

But a credit card lifestyle is not without consequences. In

the mid-1970s, Congress had to step in to regulate the credit card boom by banning the mass mailing of cards to college students and others who had not requested (and could not afford) them. As of 2005, Americans carried over $2.2 trillion in personal debt; that's over $8,000 per card-carrying household![8]

THE MERCHANTS OF COOL

The insightful PBS documentary *The Merchants of Cool* (2001) examines the industries that are passionately committed to forming consumer habits in teenagers and pre-teenagers. With massive budgets and the best of modern research techniques at their disposal, five transnational media corporations (AOL-Time Warner, Disney, Viacom, News Corporation, and General Electric) control nearly 90 percent of the media outlets available to teenagers in the United States[9] (and an estimated 75 percent worldwide). Robert McChesney, author of *Rich Media, Poor Democracy: Communication Politics in Dubious Times,* explains it this way:

> You should look at it like the British empire or the French empire in the 19th-century. Teens are like Africa. It's this range that they're gonna take over and their weaponry are films, music, books, CDs, Internet access, clothing, amusement parks, sports teams. That's all this weaponry they have to make money off of this market, to colonize this market. And that's exactly how they approach it. So they look at music as just one small part of it. They aren't music companies; they're money-making companies. And music is a weapon that generates money for them.[10]

With $150 billion in "disposable income" at stake in the United States (the estimate of what is spent annually by teens or for teens),[11] it's not just that these companies study the teenage consumption habits, but they pay millions in advertising, product placement, image making, script writing, etc. to manufacture desires and turn wants into needs. In short, millions are spent every year *manufacturing teenagers* (and the rest of us) into consumers.

It does seem as though someone's out to get us, doesn't it? It is important to realize that there is a well-organized, well-educated, focused, culture-shaping machine out there reaching for you and your money, and they aren't going to take no for an answer. Look around you. Their words and phrases are everywhere, giving opportunity after opportunity to spend your way to the image you want—the image they told you to want.

By this point you may be asking yourself, "I thought this was a book about justice—what does consumerism have to do with justice?" In a word, everything. For the Christian, justice is about how we live and how that affects those around us. Living in a "buy-now" culture is trying to re-direct what we live for and distract us from godly values. Serving the god of consumerism is one of the hidden obstacles that we have to overcome before we will be ready to live justly.

THE PROPHETIC IMAGINATION

Given the powerful infrastructure committed to manufacturing our desires and habits, we will need a deep godly influence to counter these challenges. We will also need a set of disciplines that embody hopeful alternatives. In short, we need an imagination similar to those of the ancient, Old Testament prophets, who were God's voice of critique in their present circumstances, pointing out the dangers of straying from God's ways. They also verbally painted the pictures of the hopeful possibilities of the life God dreams for His people.

This imagination—we'll call it the prophetic imagination—is required for those who are going to do the work of justice today. We are going to mention this prophetic imagination several times in this book—it is a key ingredient to living justice.

We often make the mistake of believing that the Old Testament prophets only predicted the future. In reality, as the mouthpieces of God, they spoke to and critiqued the culture around them. In other words, if you were to take a prophet to the race track with you, he or she wouldn't predict the winning horse for you. Instead he or she would be quick to point out the woes of gambling—how addictions to things like that are destructive to people, families, and societies.

Prophets, because of their ability to see and discern, not only practiced a prophetic imagination that communicated the consequences of sin, but it also communicated God's hope for restoration. In order to live lives of justice, you and I must learn to nurture this same prophetic imagination. A prophetic imagination will help us think and dream of a community that does not follow the values of this world. A prophetic imagination will help us see clearly and critically the signs of the times and help us discover more hopeful way of being—ways that God has already made possible in Jesus.

When you claim to have a prophetic imagination, you need to be careful to not distort the meaning of the word "prophet." In our culture, it's all too easy to claim the prophetic role as a form of ambition and power. It's all too easy to claim to speak prophetically, but to do so with arrogance, anger, and selfish motives.

A truly prophetic voice, however, speaks in love, not anger. Jeremiah spent 40 years telling the people, sometimes in the harshest and coarsest language possible, that they were sinners and they were going to die. But, he took no joy in that message.

As he told the people they were going to die for their sins, he had tears in his eyes.

It is this loving prophetic voice and this ability to imagine how God's love could transform the world that helps us think differently. It allows us to imagine a different way to think about possessions, and a different way to think about being a citizen.

LURED BY THE GOD OF THE HOMELAND

Jamie (co-author of this book) grew up as a missionary kid in South Africa. His story will help us understand better the next temptation—to be a citizen first.

In South Africa, I attended the local schools, learned one of the local languages, made friends, and worked hard at my school work. In many ways going to school in South Africa during the 1980s was just like going to school anywhere else in the world. Kids sat in classes with strict teachers, homework was hard, recess was fun, bullies were rarely challenged, boys and girls teased each other, and at assembly everyone sang *"Die Stem,"* the Afrikaans version of the South African national anthem. (Afrikaans is one of the languages of South Africa)

Now you might think that the only thing that distinguished my school experience in South Africa from a similar experience in the United States was singing the South African national anthem instead of saying the "Pledge of Allegiance." But there was another very significant difference. I went to school only with other white, Afrikaans speaking children. Our school was located in a town in the middle of a farming valley where whites owned all of the fertile farming land, all the property, and all of the significant businesses. Whites also controlled the local town council and ran the local police force. Not only was the school racially segregated, but it had many times the resources that all of the black schools in the surrounding area had combined.

Being white in South Africa at the time had the privileges of the white system. It was built to intentionally maintain privileges for those who were white. Governed under a system known as Apartheid (the Afrikaans word for "separateness") until 1994, all of South Africa was oppressively divided into haves and have-nots; whites have, others have not. Remember that this was in a country where at most only one-tenth of the population was white. Apartheid assigned every baby from birth to a rigid population group which determined where he or she could live and go to school, what public bathroom he or she could use, and whom he or she could marry.

Schools were segregated. Transportation was segregated. Hospitals and clinics were segregated. Beaches were segregated. Public parks were segregated. Concert halls were segregated. Restaurants were segregated. Neighborhoods were segregated. Churches were segregated.

Christianity itself often served as a way to support the reasons behind Apartheid. Christian preachers often supported Apartheid from their pulpits. Faithful white church members saw no contradiction between their worship on Sunday and the racial privileges secured for themselves (and denied others) that governed the rest of their week. Few whites questioned the comfortable combination of loyalty to the church and loyalty to the government of the day.

Most of the white Christians in South Africa were lulled by privilege into a comfortable alliance between their Christianity and their citizenship in their Apartheid homeland. Privilege has a way of diminishing the prophetic imagination. We were also chastened by our fear into blind obedience to the ruling authorities. Fear has a way of silencing the prophetic voice.

Instead of finding ourselves shaped by Christ's lessons in the parable of the Good Samaritan, instead of living in solidarity (a "by your side" kind of unity) with those who suffer, instead of living a life of compassion (suffering with those who suffer), white Christians often found it difficult to believe that the government could be as evil as their black brothers and sisters (fellow Christians) were telling us it was. We all too readily believed the news media that regularly fed us the government sactioned version of events. We all too readily believed the government rhetoric that any resistance to its benevolent policies was an act of terrorism. We were also all too ready to allow the government forces to use violence in defense of our way of life. We were conditioned to think in very narrow terms about who was included in "our" way of life.

As white Christians in South Africa, we lacked the prophetic imagination to discern more clearly the truth of the day. We lacked the prophetic imagination to act in a manner more consistent with our Christianity than the laws and conventions of our Apartheid homeland. We lacked the prophetic imagination to envision a truly more hopeful way of being the Body of Christ in the world together. We lacked the prophetic imagination to live the truth that "in Christ Jesus you are all children of God through faith. As many of you as were baptized into Christ have clothed yourselves with Christ. There is no longer Jew or Greek, there is no longer slave or free, there is no longer male and female; for all of you are one in Christ Jesus" (Galatians 3:26-28, TNIV).

GOD AND COUNTRY

If we are Christian, then our primary role is not citizens of a particular country. Our loyalty to Christ and role as witnesses to God's love should be the first of our priorities. Just like Christians in South Africa, Christians in the United States and Canada have been lulled by our privilege into a comfortable alliance between our faith and our citizenship. But what if our love of country hindered our love for those in other countries? What if God's call to "love one another" included those outside of our borders? What if it included those within our borders—but who were of a different "social group," race, or didn't have as much money as we have?

How would you answer these questions: Are you an American who happens to be a Christian, or are you a Christian who happens to be an American? Which are you first? What are you at the deepest level? In other words, to which are you *most* loyal, the nation or the way of Christ? If they ever were to come into conflict, which would you choose—your citizenship or your Christianity?

We're not saying that loyalty is wrong. On the contrary, God created us with the capacity for loyalty and faithfulness, even pride in our "people." But isn't there a problem when we give our allegiance to anyone but God? Hear us clearly on this point—there's no sin in loving your country and wanting to commit to it. But in the process, we must be careful about replacing our Christian perspectives with national perspectives.

Think of all the subtle ways that we mix the two and blend our allegiance. In the United States, we "pledge allegiance to the flag" as children. In many churches we have the American flag standing in the sanctuary (as a sentry to remind us of our citizenship). Where are the flags of all the other countries where Jesus is "King of kings"?

Have we ever considered that our commitments to country might limit our thinking of God's love for the whole world—including other nations? Have we thought of ourselves first and foremost as members of an arbitrary geography (a place defined by lines on maps) that has existed for only the last few hundred years, instead of thinking of ourselves as a global body of Christ's disciples?

We aren't suggesting that you should hate your country. We aren't suggesting that there is no place for national loyalty in the heart of a believer. But we are stating, without apology, that we are called to be members of the Body of Christ, and as such, all other loyalties are secondary. Rather than trying to juggle or balance loyalties, Christians are called to view the world and all people in it through the eyes of Christ. Our national view of the world should be shaped by God's global love.

There are some who may struggle with this idea—to them, being a citizen and being a Christian go hand-in-hand. American Christians face this more than most, because for some of them, there is a strong pride in their country and a strong belief that part of what it means to be an American is to be Christian. They see America as a Christian nation, the "good guys," who police the world. To them we can only remind them that God is a global God—Lord of heaven and earth, and His kingdom knows no boundaries. God so loved the world—not just the United States, and God doesn't favor the political country of the U.S.A. more or less than any other nation.

For others, there is a more subtle temptation. It is the temptation to split our lives in two and reconcile our love for God and love for country by compartmentalizing the two. We make sense of any conflict between loyalties by splitting up areas of our lives—we rationalize that there is no connection between the two.

SPLITTING OURSELVES

Consider again Jamie's life as a Christian in South Africa in the 1970s and 80s. Some of the most brutal racists who worked for the government were some of the most loyal members of the Dutch Reformed Church, deeply committed to their local communities and profoundly loving toward their families and fellow church members. For example, men were able to justify being loving, faithful husbands and fathers at home (and in their churches) while on the job as national security police they treated their black neighbors in savage ways. They lived this way by compartmentalizing their lives into a private sphere where their Christian commitments could rule and a public sphere where the demands of their faith took second place to the demands of their own racial/ethnic community and homeland. This compartmentalization justified violent, profoundly unchristian acts against fellow creations of God, even fellow members of the Body of Christ.

Yet maintaining this version of the private/public divide meant that we never could be reconciled with our brothers and sisters across racial lines. Obeying the rules of Apartheid competed directly with the more profound life we were called to as the Body of Christ.

Christ's call to the life of holiness is a call to bring all aspects of our lives under His lordship; it is a call to serve Him in the new Kingdom that He has already established here on earth. Our attempts to balance private Christian commitments and practices with competing public priorities won't work. We end up allowing the national priorities to govern our actions. Christian formation then becomes increasingly ineffective, influencing only our "spiritual side"—our souls, minds, or spirits—while our physical bodies—our actions—are controlled by other dominant cultural forces. This is a false split of our selves. We are made whole—body, soul, and spirit. To try to separate them is to make us something less than what we were created to be.

When we make Christian principles and practices only personal and private, it keeps us from seeing the community connectedness between us and our brothers and sisters from around the globe. If we stop seeing ourselves as part of the global body of Christ, it allows us see ourselves more as loyal citizens or loyal customers than as the family of God. It becomes easier for us to justify the exploitation of others around the world for our own gain when we do not define them as part of our community.

Certain actions are consequences of a private/public divide and contribute to strengthening our belief that those two "lives" could or should be separate. For example, we may give significant time, energy, and resources to compassionate ministries, but at the same time live in gated communities and vote for politicians and policies that benefit those who have privileged status. But living justice means going deeper than that. For example, to live justly, we know that addressing issues like racism means more than just making friends with someone who is not like us. It may mean going as far as choosing to relocate to a diverse neighborhood or working to seek racial diversity in our congregations—in order to be a living witness to Christ's attempt to reconcile us to each other.

We are first and foremost members of the Body of Christ, a global Christian community that has the authority to form our hearts, minds, and spirits. But our connection to the global body of Christ also has the authority to form our public actions and practices as well. The Body of Christ is a community that should form us not merely as individuals, but as members called to common practices—the life of holiness in the kingdom of God.

Through Christ, God initiated a new Kingdom. This new Kingdom demands a new allegiance. It demands loyalty to the God who calls us to a new kind of community—a community where the separation of our lives into a public and a private division no longer makes sense. In this new community we are called to a new integrated life.

There is a way to rethink how Christ should shape both our private *and* public activities. Once we have recognized our fundamental commitment to membership in the Body of Christ, we can begin to recognize the Body of Christ as an active body. This Body changes the way we think about using influence and resources. It claims allegiance to Christ and commits to participating fully as God builds His kingdom. Our activity together may be political in the sense that we organize our influence and resources to meet the priorities of this new Kingdom. In this new Kingdom the last shall be first; the widows, orphans, and strangers will be given special care; what we do for the least of these is what we do for Christ. As part of this body, we allow the Prince of Peace to work in our midst through love and forgiveness.

The use of power in solidarity with those who are on the margins is a witness to Christ's power at work in the world. But lest you think this is a heroic move, or seek to take pride in your attempts to be in solidarity with those who suffer, remember that Christ's solidarity with those who suffer led Him to death on the Cross.

CHAPTER 3

GOD'S ECONOMY—
GOOD NEWS TO THE POOR,
RECOVERY OF SIGHT
FOR THE BLIND

You are going to see the phrase "God's Economy" quite a bit in this chapter. Without a good concept of the economics of the Kingdom and the implications it has for all of us, any effort or conversation about justice would lack direction and purpose.

You may not care at all about economics. (Economics means, "the science that deals with the production, distribution, and consumption of goods and services, or the material welfare of humankind.")[12] That's OK; we are going to be talking about a different kind of economics here anyway. (Our interest is God's way of taking care of the welfare of humankind.) If you like economics, you may have jumped ahead and are already asking questions like these: Is God a capitalist? A socialist? A communist? What is His chosen economic policy? Which policy is the most Christian? Unfortunately, the answers to these questions are not that easy. Regardless of the dominant economic system in your town and country, you can fully participate in God's economy. And God seems to have strong economic opinions.

Here's a brief explanation: in the Bible, the people of God, known as Israel, stand in shock as they watch the waters of the Red Sea collapse on the entire Egyptian army who had been chasing them. As soon as the waters return to their original shape, the people begin to celebrate their freedom. For the first time, they are a free nation. Actually, they aren't much of a nation; rather, they are a disorganized, ragged bunch of former slaves who have been dreaming of freedom but not necessarily planning for it. In fact, they had to work hard to get organized as a people and a society that would support and nurture life for all.

But God didn't leave them all alone. He guided them—giving them the Ten Commandments as a gift from His heart. He wanted to help the Israelites organize themselves in ways that would nurture and support life in community. By following these commands, the Israelites would reflect God to the other nations. In the way they nurtured and cared for each other, they would be the image of God.

The laws against murder, adultery, and stealing were all understood as instructions for the community. In other words, God prohibits murder because by protecting the life of another person we demonstrate a part of what it means to belong to Him— to be a part of His covenant community. (They were a "covenant community" because God had made a contract, or covenant, with the Israelites to be their God, and they would be His people. The covenant with God was the basis of their reason for being together in the first place.)

But before we re-read the commandments through the lens of covenant community, let's talk about some of the other guidelines given to Israel as they were organized into a godly people. God did, in fact, suggest a few specific economic instructions to help provide and care for the Israelites. As the people of God, the Israelites were to practice:

- **Saving**. They were told not to eat all of their food or spend all of their money. Instead, they were to keep back a portion of their stock in order to prepare for leaner times. Although scholars disagree as to the percentage that should be stored away and saved, most believe you should save anywhere from 15-20 percent of your intake or income, each year. This stands in stark contrast to our shopping-driven consumer culture.

- **Tithing.** The people of God were to give back to God. Tithing was not only an act of worship and gratitude, but was also a way to protect and nurture the entire society. Again, this concept makes very little sense today when most seek to accumulate and hoard their wealth.

- **Gleaning.** While the Israelites were expected to utilize their whole land for planting, they were only supposed to harvest a portion of that land. They were to leave the edges of the fields unharvested so travelers (or animals) would have something to eat when passing through. Again, this concept sounds crazy to us. Leave a part of my field unharvested? Turn my back on potential profits? Worry about travelers and animals? But what sounds like lunacy to us was the way the Israelites went about having a caring, covenantal society.

- **Sabbath.** God commanded a Sabbath time not just for the Israelites but also for their land. For six years, the Israelites could plant and harvest but on the seventh year they were to rest and rejuvenate and plant nothing. Most of us are probably thinking that we couldn't afford a whole year without making money, but the Israelites were prepared because God had also commanded them to save. They understood the value of not being ruled or defined by a financial resource bottom line. They understood the regenerative power of rest.

- **Jubilee.** In the Old Testament, every 50th year was to be a year of jubilee. In a jubilee year, all debts were canceled.

Financial slaves were freed and were allowed to return to their lives and families. Family land, given up as payment on a debt, was given back and the debt erased. Freedom and covenant reigned supreme over the dangerous goals of a money-driven society. Of all the policies just mentioned, perhaps this one would seem the craziest to us in our culture that is so closely connected to credit cards and where living with debt is commonplace. What if next year, all of your family's debt was canceled? How much would it change your lives? (Would you immediately spend the extra money you no longer owed or would you save it?)

One thing is clear: All of these instructions demonstrate the nature and character of the society God desires and intends for us—a society that nurtures, protects, and preserves all of life.

All that we are, all that we have, and all that we produce is a gift from God. He is the Source of everything. Because we have experienced the grace of God, we should be extremely thankful people. Our worship is a way to express that thanksgiving.

But worship in God's economy is not very familiar to us. It may take further explanation—particularly on the principle of jubilee.

THE YEAR OF OUR LORD'S FAVOR: JUBILEE

Keeping the Sabbath was not just about setting aside a day of rest for some practical reason (like a farmer allowing the land to remain untouched one year so that it may replenish its nutrients). It was fundamentally about the importance of being dependant upon God's abundance and not exploiting His blessings.

As one of the Ten Commandments, keeping the Sabbath holy became a central part of the shared life of the people of God.

They, like God, were to rest on the seventh day, allowing no one—sons, daughters, slaves, or livestock—to work on that day (Exodus 20:8-11).

The concept of jubilee grows out of the Sabbath day. God commanded Moses to tell the people that not only were they to observe a weekly Sabbath, but every seven years they should observe a complete year of Sabbath where they would not work their lands (Leviticus 25:1-7). In addition, every 50 years they were to observe a special year of jubilee:

> In addition, you must count off seven Sabbath years, seven sets of seven years, adding up to forty-nine years in all. Then on the Day of Atonement in the fiftieth year, blow the ram's horn loud and long throughout the land. Set this year apart as holy, a time to proclaim freedom throughout the land for all who live there. It will be a jubilee year for you, when each of you may return to the land that belonged to your ancestors and return to your own clan. This fiftieth year will be a jubilee for you. During that year you must not plant your fields or store away any of the crops that grow on their own, and don't gather the grapes from your unpruned vines. It will be a jubilee year for you, and you must keep it holy. But you may eat whatever the land produces on its own. In the Year of Jubilee each of you may return to the land that belonged to your ancestors.
>
> When you make an agreement with a neighbor to buy or sell property, you must never take advantage of each other. When you buy land from your neighbor, the price of the land should be based on the number of years since the last jubilee. The seller will charge you only for the crop years left until the next Year of Jubilee. The more the years, the higher the price; the fewer the years, the lower the price. After all, the person

selling the land is actually selling you a certain number of harvests. Show your fear of God by not taking advantage of each other. I, the LORD, am your God (Leviticus 25:8-17, NLT).

The wealth redistribution of jubilee, and the whole idea of "Sabbath economics" may seem completely alien to us. After all, we are used to corporate businesses and consumer lifestyles that say, "Do anything you can to get more money and buy more things." However, completely resting and relying on God is an important faith principle. So is the idea of "never taking advantage of each other" in our communities—even if that means canceling debts and returning land to those who lost it. The intention of this idea was so that everyone could provide for their families. Even if they fell to hard times, once every generation there was a chance for their family to regain what was lost. Families that had been separated would be restored. Slaves were set free. Debts were canceled. Basic needs for living were restored. These ideas were (and are) fundamental building blocks of any people who would call themselves the people of God. The jubilee year was the most special year—it was a complete and hopeful change from any selfish pattern of living or economic system that hurt members of the community.

Some of you may be wondering about this idea of jubilee. You might be thinking, "How are we supposed to live out jubilee today? Is my family supposed to give our house back to the people who owned it before us?" Well, not quite—but don't miss the principle here. Jubilee is a God-given idea that is based on a loving justice. It was a way for God to say to His people, "Don't build your life around gaining lots of money or property—especially if that means doing it by exploiting or hurting those around you. These things are only temporary, and to remind you of that, every 50 years we are going to adjust things so that everyone is taken care of. Those who faced difficult times will be able to celebrate, knowing that I and My people will care for them. Don't fill up your life with temporary things—remember that I am trying to build you into a lasting community that loves each other above all else."

So if you gave your house back to the previous owners, it may not help anyone (if all of their needs are already cared for, and they are not a yet part of God's loving community, they may just hoard a gift like that, which serves no one). The principle here is that no one should be exploited, enslaved, or left alone without any way of caring for his or her family. Money can mean power, so God designed a way so that those with resources could not permanently take advantage of those who had none. This community of God's people should be focused on caring for each other's needs, not focused on getting more and more for themselves at the expense of others.[13]

The ideas of jubilee and "Sabbath economics" are embedded in the core of Jesus' life and teachings. After 40 days and nights of grueling soul searching and deep temptation, Jesus was filled with the Spirit of God and began teaching in the synagogues of Galilee. It is here that He defines the character of His coming ministry.

When he came to the village of Nazareth, his boyhood home, he went as usual to the synagogue on the Sabbath and stood up to read the Scriptures. The scroll containing the messages of Isaiah the prophet was handed to him, and he unrolled the scroll to the place where it says:

"The Spirit of the Lord is upon me,

for he has appointed me to preach Good News to the poor.

He has sent me to proclaim

that captives will be released,

that the blind will see,

that the downtrodden will be freed from their oppressors,

and that the time of the Lord's favor has come."

He rolled up the scroll, handed it back to the attendant, and sat down. Everyone in the synagogue stared at him intently. Then he said, "This Scripture has come true today before your very eyes!" (Luke 4:16-21, NLT).

Here Jesus announces His prophetic ministry on earth. And He describes His ministry in the language of jubilee! The ministry of Jesus is going to be about Good News for the poor, captives being released, freedom from oppression, and a time of favor from God—the very things described that would take place in the year of jubilee. Quoting from the prophet Isaiah (chapter 61), Jesus announces that His ministry will usher in the era of jubilee for all people.

Jesus is our jubilee. The "year of the Lord's favor," the jubilee year, where debts were canceled has happened for us in Jesus Christ. He "forgives us our debts," as it says in the Lord's Prayer, and sets us free from the oppression from sin. We can celebrate every day the way that God's people used to celebrate every fifty years. But if we think of jubilee *only* in spiritual terms, we have missed much of what Jesus lived and taught. Part of what it means to be His followers is to care for others by caring for their needs—spiritual or material. Part of what Jesus meant when He read from Isaiah was that He was there to bring God's loving justice to us. That is what He meant when He instructed His followers to "love your neighbor."

Imagine living in this "upside-down kingdom"[14] where justice and love are the primary goals of economics and forgiveness is the main form of politics. Imagine living in a world where the poor and the marginalized are blessed, the weak become strong, and the last are first.

Unfortunately, it is difficult to imagine this upside-down kingdom because we are so easily seduced into thinking that the way of our dominant culture is the way things are meant to be. It is very easy for us to say, "We know it's not the kingdom of God, but it's the best economic system out there." As followers of Jesus, it is not our place to ask, "Is this realistic?" We are to ask, "How is God's will being done on earth?" And where we don't see His will being done, we are to pray that His kingdom would come to that place, and follow His lead.

IMPLICATIONS OF SABBATH ECONOMICS FOR ONE GRANDMOTHER

If we began to imagine what God's economy might look like, we would begin to see the possibilities for a different way of living. For example, let's walk for a moment with a woman, who by the standards of our culture, is on the margins—an outsider to the benefits of North American economic systems.

Maria (not her real name) exists on low-wage jobs, usually working more than one job at a time in order to survive. She has been a janitor, a retail salesperson, and a housekeeper. Currently she is looking for a new place to live. Her new landlord has decided to raise the rent and the new rent is well beyond Maria's means. Even though her brother lives with her and shares paying the bills, they will soon have to find a new place to live or risk becoming homeless. Her children and grandchildren are not in a position to help her.

However, Maria is not worried; she has an explicit trust that God is going to take care of her. She is not bitter toward the new landlord for raising the rent nor is she bitter toward the janitorial company that had to downsize and let her go. She believes that no matter what, God will take care of her.

The implications of Maria's confidence in God for meeting her needs are complex. The beauty of such a profound faith is that Maria is indeed sustained by it even when there is not enough money to put food on the table. Her faith leads her to give of her time at food kitchens and homeless shelters despite the fact that she herself has never been far from poverty. In some ways, her faith shelters her from the harsh realities in her life.

Yet the faith Maria places in God makes her less likely to be critical of those who are partly responsible for the harsh economic realities in her life. She cannot control prevailing wages or the rising cost of housing, but there are people who can. Employers and city leaders have a responsibility to secure a living wage and more affordable housing for workers like Maria.

Maria does not have the time or energy to fight for a living wage; she is too busy working just to make ends meet. To see permanent changes to her circumstances, she would have to rely on fellow Christians—those who have privilege and opportunity. Those who have resources and a voice would need to speak up. In fact if they did, it would be very consistent with God's economy—the principles He established with Sabbath and jubilee.

Although living under the assumptions of consumer values would have us think otherwise, people and houses are not meant to be bought and sold for selfish greed. Livable wages and affordable housing are more than cogs in an economic machine; they are the foundations for building sustainable lives, families, and communities.

The call to just wages is not only for employers and city leaders; it is deeply embedded within Christian traditions. In Deuteronomy 24, the people of God are commanded to "Never take advantage of poor and destitute laborers, whether they are fellow Israelites or foreigners living in your towns. You must pay them their wages each day before sunset because they are poor and are counting on it" (vv. 24:14-15*a*).

REFUSING TO BUY IT: LIVING JUSTICE AS A WAY OF LIFE

A Christian way of life is not based on the same values you would find in a society based on shopping and consuming. Christianity is based on abundant grace for all; consumer culture rewards individual achievement. Christianity assumes God has provided enough for everyone if we will share; consumer culture says that we must compete for scarce resources. In Christianity, sharing of resources among the community is important; consumerism says that private wealth accumulation is the goal. Christianity is a life that seeks to love God and each other; consumerism is a life that seeks to fulfill made-up desires through the purchase of new products. Christianity takes seriously the reality of sin and selfishness but believes that God overcame sin in Christ and is in the process of repairing the rift; a consumer driven society takes seriously the reality of sin and selfishness and seeks to capitalize on it.

Consumer culture in North America is the dominant culture. It cuts across most if not all sub-cultures and molds our character. It seeks to shape us into placing a high value on things like individual achievement, competitiveness, productivity, efficiency, self-sufficiency, youth, the "cutting edge," and satisfying our desires. Each of these values, may at first seem harmless or even desirable. However, when these are drummed into our heads every day by store sale signs and advertisements telling us to "buy, buy, buy," these values distract us from living the life of holiness to which we are called as the Body of Christ. But there is another way.

THE LIFE OF HOLINESS AS CHRIST'S ALTERNATIVE TO CONSUMER CULTURE

Christians living in North America have been deeply shaped by consumer culture—to the point that shopping values have invaded the church. Mega-churches market to "spiritual shoppers." Church leaders often stress growth in church attendance/membership and financial contributions as the principal markers of a successful church—just like the business corporations that sell products and produce profits. People wearing Left Behind t-shirts and WWJD bracelets and other trinkets, also shop around for churches—ones that serve their needs with pastors who "feed them." Children sing their favorite Veggie Tales songs while carrying their Precious Moments Bibles to church. A quick jaunt through any Christian Bookstore reveals how far-reaching consumer culture is. The Christian consumer has become a moneymaking target for sellers.

Christians living in North America have never been completely taken over by the culture of consumption. Some try to be frugal in their lifestyles and avoid over the top luxury spending. Many give generously to good causes and people in need. Many are more concerned with the value that they find in their work than with how much it pays. "Many devote time they could use to make more money (or enjoy spending) in volunteer work in the church and for other causes. Many make decisions about their work with serious consideration of how they affect personal relations and other non-economic needs within the family."[15] But in many ways, we let some of the smaller, less obvious influences of our "shopper's values" slip past our guard, and before we realize it, we have actually traded some of Christ's value system for the values of the world. And this affects our involvement in the world. We end up at a place where consumer culture has shaped our relationships, desires, and habits, often in ways that move us away from a life of holiness. But the good news is that by the grace of God and the help of Christ, we can resist the corrupting forces of consumer culture. Christ's call to the life of holiness restores our values by reshaping the way we relate to each other and by re-creating our desires and habits.

RESHAPING THE WAY WE RELATE TO EACH OTHER

The values of the consumer culture are dependent upon turning people into self-interested individuals. Christ's call to the life of holiness requires that we "turn the camera around." We don't focus the lens on ourselves in self-interest, seeing life as a play about us and what we can get for ourselves. Instead, we turn the camera upon the world—and see ourselves as participants in God's drama about the Body of Christ loving the world as God does.

Christ's call to the life of holiness challenges us to develop the art of giving and receiving, not the art of the sale. When we are trained to serve customers we know it is ultimately for the profit of the business. Customer service itself is ultimately something for our own gain, whether that be workers' wages or company profit. We sometimes use this same kind of "exchange" language when we volunteer our time in "service" to the church or community. However, we are not called to "provide service" but to love and give freely of all that we have and all that we are. God's gift of Christ on the Cross was not a service that somehow met Christ's needs while meeting ours; it was the ultimate gift of love without the possibility of return. Christ calls us to follow Him by loving others in the same way.

RE-CREATING OUR DESIRES

Consumer culture survives by constantly changing (or refashioning) our desires. Advertisers try to sell us more than products. They are selling desires. They show us commercials telling us that we want to be liked by the opposite sex—then they show us how their deodorant will help us get it. "Friendship, intimacy, love, pride, happiness and joy are actually the *objects* we buy and consume, much more so than the tubes, liquor bottles, Cadillacs, and Buicks that promise them and bear their names."[16]

Central to the life of holiness is the re-creation of our passions and desires. Christ changes the object of our desires, calling us to "'Love the Lord your God with all your heart and with all your soul and with all your strength and with all your mind'; and, 'Love your neighbor as yourself'" (Luke 10:27). In contrast to the "need" for pleasure and self-fulfillment, Christ calls us to nurture the passions of the Spirit. We will know that our passions are being shaped by Christ when our lives embody love, joy, peace, patience, kindness, generosity, faithfulness, gentleness, and self-control (Galatians 5:19-26).

It is easy to justify what we own and how much we spend on ourselves when we compare ourselves to others in our neighborhood or in our church who are spending just as much or more. Because everyone around us is living that way, we rise to that lifestyle—when we really could get by with much less.[17] Advertisers draw our gaze up the money ladder to those who are much richer than we are, shifting the scale we use for measuring rich and poor. (Pretty soon we think of ourselves as poor—compared to those in the gated community down the street!)

In his sermon *On Riches*, John Wesley tells a story illustrative of how conditioned we can be by our wealth:

> I was talking with a rich gentleman the other day. While we were talking, he ordered one of his servants to throw some more coals on the fire. When the servant did so, a puff of smoke came out of the fireplace toward my rich friend. My rich friend jumped back and said to me, "Mr. Wesley, these are the burdens I must deal with every day." I couldn't help asking him, "Are these the heaviest burdens with which you must deal?"[18]

John Wesley was making the point that this man thought he was so "poor" having to endure the "burden" of a puff of smoke. With his riches, that was the worst thing he had to worry about. Forgetting the real poor who struggle just to survive, he had convinced himself that his life was difficult.

Instead of allowing wealth and resources to change us, we must choose to allow God to change our way of thinking about wealth and resources. The life of holiness that Christ calls us to should lead us to identify with the poor and oppressed and to measure wealth by the poorest in our world, not the richest. Only when our desires are shaped by that perspective, will we begin to desire to see justice and love change our world.

REFORMING OUR HABITS

While advertisers spend billions trying to make us dissatisfied with who we are and what we have, 1 Timothy reminds us that "true godliness with contentment is itself great wealth. After all, we brought nothing with us when we came into the world, and we can't take anything with us when we leave it. So if we have enough food and clothing, let us be content" (vv. 6:6-

8, NLT). Contentment is hard to find in the midst of a market driven society where we are never thin enough, our teeth are never white enough, our cars are never fast enough, and our accounts are never large enough. Contentment can only come in the midst of a community that lives in the abundance of God's grace. Such a community will be instrumental in shaping not only our desires but our habits as well. Those "market forces" and consumer values are too powerful and pervasive to face alone. We need the support of a community based on God's values, and shaped by His abundant grace.

Think of the instruction by John Wesley in his sermon *On the Use of Money:* "Gain all you can. Save all you can. Give all you can."[19] We usually do well with the first two principles, but it is difficult to say that we have truly given *all* that we can. Again, our understanding of what this means has been influenced by the wealth and standards that surround us. When we compare ourselves to the wealthy around us, our giving looks pretty good. But if we really want to reform our habits of giving, we might instead look at the lives of the poorest around the world. It is difficult to argue that we have given all we can when one of our cars costs more than four homes in rural South Africa. It is difficult to argue that we have given all we can when we throw away more food each week than 75 percent of the world *eats* in that same week. Could it be that advertisers and marketers have conditioned us to think first about buying for ourselves than about giving to others? Could it be that our consumer mindset has shaped our habits of giving more than our Christian values of love, mercy, and justice?

When interpreting what Christ meant when He said it is harder for a rich man to enter heaven than for a camel to go through the eye of a needle, Wesley said:

As I understand it, what is meant here by "a rich person," is not only someone who has immense treasures, a person that has heaped up gold as dust, and silver as the sand of the sea; but anyone who possesses more than the necessities and conveniences of life. A person who has food and clothing sufficient for themselves and their family, and some left over, is rich.[20]

Since we live in neighborhoods where gated communities and zoning laws carefully shield us from the poor even in our own towns, we will have to be very intentional about placing our lives (and our help) among those who are poor.

As the apostle Paul exhorted the Galatians, "Do not use your freedom to indulge the sinful nature; rather serve one another in love" (Galatians 5:13). It would be difficult to conceive of accumulating wealth if we saw our lives intimately connected to the lives of all Christians around the world. The call to the life of holiness is a call to live as a holy people, a people who "share with God's people who are in need [and] practice hospitality" (Romans 12:13). Christians often think that as long as their quest for wealth does not interfere with their devotion to God, it is acceptable. But can devotion to God be divorced from our devotion to one another? Here is an important question to consider: Has God given us wealth primarily for our own use? Or has He blessed us in order to bless our community through us? As Christians we must resist the habits that have been ingrained in us by the surrounding consumer culture. We must begin to reform our habits of giving and the way we think about what we have been given. When we do, perhaps we will realize that wealth is given principally for the good of God's people, not for each individual Christian's own personal fulfillment.

While our consumer culture shapes how we relate to each

other, creates false desires, and forms our habits in ways that are often contrary to the life of holiness, there is still hope. By the grace of God we can draw from the deep resources available to us by God's Spirit and the support of a transformed Christian community to change these patterns. By the grace of God we can find new ways to use our resources for the common good. If we are faithful in this way, we will take offense at cute little shopping carts, we will expose advertising for the empty desires and habits it forms, and we will nurture Christian alternatives to the values of consumer culture.

RE-IMAGINING THE CHURCH THAT HELPS US TO RE-IMAGINE THE WORLD

A faithful Church will help us develop the vision and habits to recognize how our economic value systems (especially in the form of hyper-consumer buyer mentality) prevent us from being "one faith [and] one baptism" (Ephesians 4:5). If we are truly one faith with one baptism, the marks on our body will look like the Fruit of the Spirit: love, joy, peace, patience, kindness, goodness, gentleness, faithfulness, and self-control. They will not be the marks of hyper-consumer "buy and hoard" mentality:

- "Market"-style exchanges—which turns love into something to be bought and sold,
- Manufactured desire—which reduces joy to happiness you can buy,
- Mc-fast food consumption—which makes patience obsolete,
- Self-sufficiency—which makes kindness seem unnecessary,
- Self-help—which makes goodness irrelevant,
- Planned obsolescence (where companies make products so that they will break or no longer function in the fu-

ture—so that you will have to buy new ones from them again and again)[21]—which makes faithfulness unfashionable,

- Aggressive accumulation—which makes gentleness seem like a weakness, and
- Preying on addictions—which makes self-control next to impossible.[22]

Our faith calls for a community that can practice an economy that "stands in contrast to (and offers a salvation from) an economics of scarcity, consumption, greed, utility, and competition."[23]

There is much to confess when we realize that we have helped the powers and principalities that are constantly at work seeking to divide the Body of Christ and prevent reconciliation with God and each other. But in Christ, God has already established His reign. The reconciliation has already been made possible. Signs of the Kingdom are all around us. God is renewing our prophetic imagination. He is helping us to see our world the way the prophets of old saw it—seeing past the lies that have deceived us—and seeing God's hope and love for the world. God is giving us new eyes to see and ears to hear. We believe we are at a moment when God is calling the Church to nurture the prophetic imagination.[24]

CHAPTER 4
A CHOSEN PEOPLE–
CHRISTIAN BEFORE
CITIZEN

In 2002, Jamie co-facilitated a mission trip to Tecate, Mexico:

On this trip, we did not play soccer with neighborhood kids, lead a Vacation Bible School, build anything, do street evangelism, show a Jesus film, serve in a soup kitchen, or preach the gospel; instead, we were dedicated to listening.

While there, we asked a group of pastors to talk about the difficult aspects of receiving so many gringo mission teams. ("Gringo" is a Mexican slang term meaning those from the privileged North who are citizens of the United States or Europe; it is most often associated with some variation of white skin and culture.) These teams came regularly from "El Otro Lado" (literally "the other side" in Spanish).

One of the pastors smiled when we used the term "gringo." He recognized that we were being confessional, but he said that not all of the teams that come from El Otro Lado were in fact gringo, only the ones who wouldn't listen.

Perhaps the most truthful and prophetic comments about listening came from the caretaker of the campgrounds where we slept. While showing us the leaky pipes and cracked walls, he talked about his difficulty in getting parts from El Otro Lado for the new showers (put in by a mission team) in the cinderblock dormitories. Through this discussion, he made the uneven reality of the border come alive—parts and people can flow south across the border almost at will, but crossing the border north for even the most mundane of needs is a monumental task.

This difficulty in crossing the border makes working with mission teams challenging. He explained that there are a lot of talented people with construction experience and expensive tools that come to help out. But because of the dynamics that make it difficult for him to get supplies, he's hesitant to use those latest and greatest technologies. Instead, he often chooses to use the simpler techniques and technology because it will be easier to fix or replace after all the talent and tools leave.

Most mission teams understand this fact and respect the way things must be done in Tecate. However, occasionally there are teams that just won't listen or who won't do things the way they need to be done in Tecate. For those teams, the caretaker has a solution—he has them build a wall on a slab of concrete in the middle of a courtyard. They feel as if they are accomplishing something great, but once they have left, the caretaker tears it down and gets it ready for the next group that has too much to give and not enough time or patience to listen and learn.

Upon hearing this story, we dubbed the wall the "gringo wall"; we realized it represented our inability to listen to one another. It became a symbol of how the borders of our homelands too often determine the boundaries of our identity and actions more than our membership in the Body of Christ.

CITIZENS OF A HIGHER ALLEGIANCE; PEOPLE OF MERCY

Borders mess with our categories of "us and them"; they tempt us to place others in categories that are not consistent with the fellowship we are called to in Christ. Because of borders we are more likely to think that others are less deserving of our concern, charity, and compassion.

As an alternative, consider what the apostle Peter wrote to the Christians living in what is modern-day Turkey. The books of 1 and 2 Peter are addressed to Christians living as aliens and exiles in five very different provinces of Asia Minor. Although all five provinces were part of the Roman Empire, the Christians there were converts from very different people groups with different local economies, religions, and languages.

Because of their beliefs, they were being harassed and persecuted, so Peter tries to encourage them: "You are a chosen people, a royal priesthood, a holy nation, a people belonging to God, that you may declare the praises of him who called you out of darkness into his wonderful light. Once you were not a people, but now you are the people of God; once you had not received mercy, but now you have received mercy. Dear friends, I urge you, as aliens and strangers in the world, to abstain from sinful desires, which war against your soul" (1 Peter 2:9-11).

It is not their status as citizens in the Roman Empire that makes them a people. It is not their language or their local geography that makes them a people. It is not their ethnicity, race, or heritage that makes them a people. It is the fact that they have received God's mercy. It is the fact that they are a people responding to God's grace, a people called to "proclaim the mighty acts of the Lord" (Psalm 106:2).

This is the heart of the matter. As Christians we are a worshiping body first, and citizens after. If we are not careful and we get those two confused, we can easily allow others to tell us what Christians should do in the world. It is like two teams on the soccer field. If we are proud and cheering for our team, we can get caught up in it. We don't appreciate a good play by the other team when they make a good effort or score a goal. If one of our players knocks down and hurts one of their players, that is too bad—but it's all part of the game. They are on the other side, and so if something bad happens to them, we don't care. What matters most is that our team can run their game plan, and that nothing stops us from winning.

In the same way, our loyalty to our country can cloud our vision of global justice for all. When it comes to our citizenship, sometimes our pride in our country keeps us from caring about those "on the other side." When this happens, we stop pursuing justice for them. It doesn't matter what happens to those who are across the border as long as our country is unaffected. If our country chooses policies and practices that may result in their harm, endanger their well-being, or exploits them, well, that is part of the game, right? But that does not represent the love of Christ. Fellow human beings and sometimes even brothers and sisters in Christ can be viewed as enemies just because they are on the other side of the border. Or if we don't see them as enemies, we don't care to act when something bad happens to them and don't seek to make sure they have all that they need.

But living justice means loving our neighbors. (It also means loving even our enemies.) As the world becomes increasingly interconnected, those halfway around the world become my neighbor. As the book of 1 John has said, "If any one of you has material possessions and sees a brother or sister in need but has no pity on them, how can the love of God be in you?" (3:17, TNIV). Sometimes we see our brothers and sisters in need on the news, and they are oceans away. But because we know about their need, we can't go on and pretend that we were unaware. The Bible calls us to love them—to take care of their need—if the love of God is truly in us.

A SUBVERSIVE WORSHIP REVOLUTION

So what happens when the instructions of Jesus and the policies of our countries are in conflict? What are we supposed to do then? The Bible has several things to say on this. First, the Bible instructs us to obey those in authority over us. This is stated in both Romans 13:1-7, and 1 Peter 2:12-17. It is important to note the context of these verses. We are called to do good and to live such good lives before those in authority over us so that we might be a witness to them. Then they would have nothing bad to say about us (and thus about our God). This was written to groups of believers who often faced persecution from non-Christian authorities. The instruction to them was not to respond with rebellion and violence, but to respond with obedience and lives so good that those in authority would have no reason to persecute or even speak badly about the body of Christ.

On the other hand, in Acts 5:17-42, Peter and the apostles are told by those in authority to stop teaching about Jesus. To this Peter replies, "We must obey God rather than human beings!" (v. 29). At this point, with the church under persecution and with the command of human authority in direct opposition to the command of God, Peter reminds us that our allegiance to God comes first. So we must balance these two ideas—we are to submit to authority for the sake of our witness and to keep from bringing needless persecution, but no matter what, our loyalty and obedience is to God.

Whether or not the authorities over us support or resist the kingdom of God, we are called to obedience and to lives that represent Christ as our true king. In some ways, it does not matter how authorities treat us, we are witnesses and ambassadors of God's love in the world. As in the instances where the Bible says that we are to submit to authority, we are instructed to live such good lives that they cannot ignore the goodness of God in their midst. Our actions are to influence and shine light on all around us—our neighbors, our country, and those beyond our borders.

One of the ways we can do this is by being the worshiping community we are called to be. As we worship God, we are witnesses and influencers of those around us. In this way, our worship is subversive. Someone who is subversive is "a radical supporter of political or social revolution."[25] We are using subversive here in a positive sense, to mean an advocate of change, who works in small, subtle ways. More on that in a moment. Our worship is subversive because it says that God exists and rules over the whole earth. When we worship Him, we are saying to any other authority that would lay claim to us that God rules our lives and all of life, first and foremost. When we worship Jesus as Lord of all, we are saying that we bow our knee to Him alone. God is first in our lives—everything else is a distant second. When we worship God we are saying that we will follow His commands and His ways for living in the world. This says to any who would rule us, "Sorry, God is in charge of my life. I worship Him alone."

WORSHIP AS SUBVERSIVE ACTS

The very act of worshiping together is a subversive act, but not in the way that saboteurs (people that blow things up in protest) are subversive. We mean subversive in the way that Walter Brueggemann describes in his book *Deep Memory, Exuberant Hope*:

> We preachers are summoned to get up and utter a *sub-version* of reality, an alternative version of reality that says another way of life in the world is not only possible, but is peculiarly mandated and peculiarly valid. It is a *sub-version* because we must fly low, stay under the radar, and hope not

to be detected too soon, a sub-version because it does indeed intend to *sub-vert* the dominant version and to empower a community of *sub-versives* who are determined to practice their lives according to a different way of imagining. [26]
Baptism, prayer, scripture reading, preaching and hearing sermons, keeping the Sabbath holy, and joining in communion (the Eucharist) are all forms of subverting the economics and the politics of our day.

By worship we mean more than the worship during the service time at church. Singing praise songs is only one part of what worship truly is. Worship includes all of the acts of the Christian church that tie us more deeply to the story of God and all that shapes us as a people to respond to grace in thanksgiving. Justice is an act of worship too. Worship means that we give time and money to help alleviate the suffering of those dying by war and oppression. Worship means sending medical supplies to prevent death at the hands of diseases that are preventable—but life threatening in places that have few resources. Worship means seeking fair trade coffee when we buy coffee, so that workers in Columbia are given fair wages and can support their families (instead of being mistreated so that North Americans can get their coffee a few cents cheaper). Worship is writing to our government to use diplomacy to intervene and prevent genocide when we hear about it happening around the world. Worship is remembering that we are aliens and strangers (or exiles) in this world (see Hebrews 11:13 and 1 Peter 2:11). Because we know what it feels like to be an outsider in this world, we go out of our way to care for the visitors and orphans in our midst.

ACTS OF WORSHIP THAT BRING CHANGE

Let's explore the different forms of worship that help us to express the justice of God.

Baptism

In John 3:5-6 Jesus says, "'I tell you the truth, no one can enter the kingdom of God unless he is born of water and the Spirit. Flesh gives birth to flesh, but the Spirit gives birth to spirit.'" Jesus, in talking about the people of God, uses family terms; He sees the use of water (baptism) as a birthplace for members of this godly family. In essence Jesus is *redefining* family, saying "Water is thicker than blood."

We see this redefinition again in Luke 8:19-21: "Now Jesus' mother and brothers came to see him, but they were not able to get near him because of the crowd. Someone told him, 'Your mother and brothers are standing outside, wanting to see you.' He replied, 'My mother and brothers are those who hear God's word and put it into practice.'"

Baptism is dangerous thing which can be used to make a statement of allegiance. You see, when people are baptized, they are publicly stating that they have chosen to be initiated into the Christian family. When people choose to be baptized, they are promising to see and live in the world in the Christian way. For many, joining this family means leaving a different family. So baptism celebrates the changing of allegiance from one family to another. In many parts of the world, this can be seen as a threat to those in authority.

In baptism, Christians are initiated into life in the Body of Christ. It is our rite of initiation into a new culture, family, and people. It is the very public and visible mark of our commitment to new loyalties—a life devoted to following Christ.

Regular Prayer and Scripture Reading

Prayer and scripture reading are also profoundly subversive acts. It is through these means that we learn the story of God and where we fit into that story. Meditating on the story of God helps us to counter the alternative stories that constantly flood our eyes and ears. Prayer and scripture reading re-center our story in the story of God, away from the story of a particular homeland, an ethnic group, or a particular socio-economic niche. Prayer and scripture reading are at the heart of being a Christian radical.

By radical we mean getting back to the roots of what it means to be Christian. In his book *The Irresistible Revolution: Living as an Ordinary Radical,* Shane Claiborne gets at the notion of radical when he confesses:

> What I often get branded is "radical." I've never really minded that, for as my urban-farming friends remind me, the word *radical* itself means "root." It's from the Latin word *radix,* which, just like a rad-ish, has to do with getting to the root of things. But radical is not something reserved for saints and martyrs, which is why I like to compliment it with *ordinary.* Ordinary does not mean normal, and I lament the dreadful seduction which has resulted in Christians becoming so normal. Thankfully, there is a movement of ordinary radicals sweeping the land, and ordinary people are choosing to live in radical new ways.[27]

The beauty in the practices of regular prayer and scripture reading is that it makes the impossible, possible. It is through prayer and Bible reading that we are changed. Through the teachings of Christ, we begin to understand and live the life of Christ. Soon we find ourselves "bearing a cross" for the poor, those hurt by violence, and those who have no one to care for them.

Preaching and Receiving Sermons

There was a time, prior to the 17th-century, when it was all but inconceivable to think of a world without God, but that is not the case now. In today's world little thought is given to how our advancements relate to life with God.

So, in a world that can so easily imagine itself without God, preaching becomes subversive. As author Walter Brueggemann says,

> In a culture that has learned well how to imagine—how to make sense—of the world without reference to the God of the Bible, it is the preacher's primal responsibility to invite and empower and equip the community to reimagine the world as though [God] were a key and decisive player.[28]

This is no easy task, and it demands we draw on our greatest intellectual and spiritual resources. Preaching is not so much about making the gospel relevant to a contemporary society as it is about helping contemporary society see beyond the lies of its time so they can behold the beauty of a life lived with God.

In addition to being politically subversive, preaching is economically subversive. It is subversive because God's good news is for the poor, the oppressed, the blind, the prisoners, and the ones trapped in debt. Preaching should call us to a different way of being in the world economically; it should call us to follow Christ and shape us into a body that cannot participate in practices that contribute to someone else's poverty.

Keeping the Sabbath Holy

Other than prayer, there is perhaps no act more central to being the people of God than keeping the Sabbath holy. Judaism has a long tradition of laws and prescriptions of how to keep the Sabbath holy. Twice, however, in his epistles, the apostle Paul made it clear that Sabbath observances, like other external signs of piety, have often been abused and are insufficient for salvation. As he wrote to the Colossians, "Do not let anyone condemn you for what you eat or drink, or for not celebrating certain holy days or new moon ceremonies, or Sabbaths. For these rules are only shadows of the reality yet to come. And Christ himself is that reality" (Colossians 2:16-17, NLT). When rebuked by the Pharisees for picking grain on the Sabbath, Jesus criticized those who forgot why Sabbath observance existed in the first place: "The Sabbath was made for man, not man for the Sabbath" (Mark 2:27).

Attention to keeping the Sabbath holy reorients our sense of time. It is the foundation of a Christian calendar that, if regularly attended, can have a profound effect on Christian discipleship. Keeping the Sabbath holy is a subversive act because it interrupts our drive to consume and exposes our obsession with keeping busy.

Keeping the Sabbath holy centers our time in God. It is the foundation for an entire Christian calendar that can help us think about time in ways very different from those demanded by the marketplace or the homeland. When we move rhythmically (liturgically) from Sabbath to Sabbath, the 40-hour work week becomes a means to an end, not an end in itself. Observing the seasons of the Christian calendar (Advent, Christmas, the Season after Epiphany, Lent, Holy Week, Easter, and Ordinary Time) can be a daily reminder that we are first citizens of the kingdom of God and operate on His timetable.

Celebrating Communion (Eucharist)

There is perhaps no act of worship more subversive in our economic and political environment than for Christians to celebrate Communion together. Celebrating Communion serves three purposes: 1) it is an act of memory; 2) it is an act of thanksgiving; and 3) it is an act that guides the prophetic imagination to a life lived in communion with God and one another.

The Eucharist should remind us that the Christian life is about more than me and my personal, intimate walk with my God. It should remind us 1) that God is a part of human history, 2) that we are all dependent on God and on each other, and 3) that we should be drawn beyond ourselves and our individual needs to consider our place alongside others in the story of God.

Unfortunately, in Protestant circles the thinking about the Eucharist doesn't get out of the intellectual or individualistic realm. Many Communion services focus almost exclusively on the individual's mediation of Christ's sacrifice. Little attention is paid to the physical and social elements of Communion.

Something that Catholic Christians have done well to remember is that the Eucharist is fundamentally about the Incarnation—God in the flesh. The Eucharist is a model for how we are to live in the world. The bread and the cup are physical elements that remind us that God is deeply concerned about our physical hunger and the ways in which we share our resources with one another. The Eucharist is a reminder that our spiritual priorities must be reflected in our material life together. Acts 2 records one of the earliest practices of Communion:

> Those who believed what Peter said were baptized and added to the church that day—about 3,000 in all. All the believers devoted themselves to the apostles' teaching, and to fellowship, and to sharing in meals (including the Lord's Supper), and to prayer. A deep sense of awe came over them all, and the apostles performed many miraculous signs and wonders. And all the believers met together in one place and shared everything they had. They sold their property and possessions and shared the money with those in need. They worshiped together at the Temple each day, met in homes for the Lord's Supper, and shared their meals with great joy and generosity—all the while praising God and enjoying the goodwill of all the people. And each day the Lord added to their fellowship those who were being saved (Acts 2:41-47, NLT).

Notice the intimate relationship between Christian discipleship and concrete material realities like eating and sharing what one has with those who may go without.

The connection between hearing the Word and living it out couldn't be clearer. Check out Acts 4:31-35:

> After they prayed, the place where they were meeting was shaken. And they were all filled with the Holy Spirit and spoke the word of God boldly. All the believers were one in heart and mind. No one claimed that any of his possessions was his own, but they shared everything they had. With great power the apostles continued to testify to the resurrection of the Lord Jesus, and much grace was upon them all. There were no needy persons among them. For from time to time those who owned lands or houses sold them, brought the money from the sales and put it at the apostles' feet, and it was distributed to anyone as he had need.

Notice that the movement of the Spirit, something we think of as thoroughly beyond this material world, had profound material consequences. Experiencing the love of God spurred these Christians to change their concept of power and to literally care for the needs among them.

Because this kind of thinking and living is so foreign to so many, and because we don't often preach that the Spirit encourages and enlivens our charity, efforts to share and redistribute are characterized in strange, funny, political, or even hateful ways. Those who share in the power of the Spirit have been labeled crazy, people-looking-for-a-tax-break, or even communists.

Yet the Spirit of God has also called us to challenge and to change the dominant economic and political reality that surrounds us. We can do that by remembering the following principles:

- The Spirit has called us to be faithful to the vision set forth in the life, teachings, death, and Resurrection of

Christ. We are to shine the light not on ourselves but on the One who makes life possible.

- The gift of the Spirit is for the sake of the entire world; however, the body of Christ has the obligation to ask what a faithful response to the love of Christ looks like. It is not a Christian's responsibility to find solutions to problems that "work for all human beings at all times and in all places." That is an impossibility that displaces God and puts humans in the place of judging (and controlling) what it good for everyone. Such an all-encompassing gaze is the false claim of the homeland. The people of God need to recognize that "now we see but a poor reflection as in a mirror; then we shall see face to face" (1 Corinthians 13:12).

- We may have political and legal systems in place that do bring justice to people; however, this cannot be equated with the fullness of God's reign. Christians should constantly subject these systems to the scrutiny of the gospel because even when we attempt to alleviate suffering, humans have the tendency to set up systems that repress as much as they liberate.

- In places where life is set up around buying and selling, we are trained to think about ourselves: our rights, our property, our resources, and our abilities. It is therefore a revolutionary act to imagine and live out a reality that is not grounded in personal choice or private profit. The gift of the Spirit allows us to creatively engage the world, living in such a way that we create a community that conforms to the Fruit of the Spirit (love, joy, peace, patience, kindness, goodness, faithfulness, gentleness, and self-control).

Finally, the Eucharist is about re-membering—becoming members once again—of the Body of Christ. It is about knitting together the followers of Christ. The Eucharist is a connector. It connects us to the depth and breadth of the Christian story; it connects us to the ancient Passover; it connects us to the suffering, death, and Resurrection of Christ. Communion, as is all worship, is inherently a formative discipline. It is a call to embody the reconciling love of God in fellowship with one another.

MOVING IN COMMUNITY

The people of God move in community, gathering for the liturgy, a word meaning "the work of the people." (Liturgy is usually used to describe the order and arrangement of worship.) The "work" of the people of God, as we have already said, is to rehearse a life of worship, remembering and reflecting the nature of God. Our liturgies tell us what God is like; they remind us of the cares and concerns of God; and they then teach us the movements involved in being the Body of Christ. Having gathered together, the people of God move together within the liturgy each Sunday: we stand up and sit down at the same times; we sing the same songs together; we listen together as the Word is preached; we celebrate and rehearse the memory of the life and death and the resurrected life of Christ in Communion; and we leave together, prepared to live in the world as Christ.

It is the dream of God that outside the walls of the sanctuary, we would continue to live as a unified Body of Christ. Having been reminded again of the mind, nature, and character of God in our church services, we now carry those same messages back to our homes, schools, places of work, and neighborhoods. And though we are scattered to many different places, the people of God continue to move in unity, living out that which we have rehearsed in the liturgy. What does this look like for justice? How can we continue to move in unity when we are no

67

longer in the same room? How do we pursue justice together as an act of worship? One way to answer these questions is to explore how the Body of Christ continues its worship in service, advocacy, and resistance.

JUSTICE THROUGH WORSHIP—OUTSIDE CHURCH WALLS

Service is a term familiar to most of us. In service we take the posture of Christ who himself took off His outer garment so as to take on the clothing of a foot-washing servant. Where the rest of the planet is concerned, Christianity is a very odd way to live because Christians move together to take the posture of servanthood, whenever and wherever a need might arise. We're not saying that Christians are the only people who serve, but as Christians—those who live the way of Jesus—we serve because it is how we have been led and shaped and rehearsed. Where there is need for service, we serve. It's who we are.

More often than not, our service is a form of advocacy. To advocate is to speak or act in support or in defense of a person, a group of people, or a cause. To serve the poor is to advocate for the poor. Feeding and caring for those who have little or nothing is a powerful act of support and protection.

But advocacy can take many different forms. For example, illiteracy is major problem in many of the neighborhoods in U.S. cities. Christians across the city advocate by participating in after-school tutoring and reading programs, but also by encouraging elected leaders (school board members, state representatives, city council members, congressional representatives) to pass legislation to repair schools, build schools, raise teacher salaries, buy more materials, and increase the safety of schools and neighborhoods.

A well-written letter sent to a congressional leader can be an act of advocacy. An opinion voiced at an open city council meeting can be an act of advocacy. Participating in a non-violent march or protest can be an act of advocacy.

Living justice requires that the Body of Christ advocate for those at the margins, those in harm's way. We are their advocates. We live and speak so as to protect, defend, and encourage people and systems to value all of life.

There is a growing movement to address global warming and other environmental concerns. Those who wish to advocate for the environment can do so by making their homes more energy efficient, by driving cars that are more fuel efficient, by encouraging local and national leaders to pass more environmentally friendly laws and policies.

You may have seen the white bracelets with the world "ONE" on them. They are the symbols and tools of the One campaign, a movement designed to advocate for the people of Africa who are being devastated by the AIDS virus. The "ONE" on these bracelets represent the wishes of the people of this movement—that the United States would set aside 1 percent of its annual budget to battle the AIDS epidemic in Africa. This is an incredibly powerful and effective movement of advocacy.

Advocacy sometimes means learning. We won't get involved in something we don't know about. For example, you may know nothing about the cause of "invisible children." If you haven't already, find and watch the videos about them—Ugandan children who are taken from their homes and forced to fight in a civil war. There is a growing movement that seeks to raise money to find and liberate these children while pressuring government leaders to end this bloody conflict. Those who join this movement become powerful advocates for those who don't have the power to stand up for themselves.

Learn, study, read. Find out all you can about the subject and the many different ways you might be able to serve and advocate well.

But what do we do when these efforts don't work? What do we do when we are confronted by systems and situations that continue to hurt or exploit? As we have already said, we serve those hurt by these same systems, and then we advocate for them in the hopes that policies or procedures can be changed for the better. But after that, when unhealthy situations continue to do harm and when no one will listen, we resist.

This is a very difficult concept, one that has to be discussed and undertaken with great wisdom and much prayer. And most importantly, we must remember that as we resist, we remain members of the Body of Christ, people of the way of Christ. Our resistance must always remind those watching of the Christ who willingly gave himself in the most non-violent of ways.

So what can resistance look like? What does it look like today? Here are a few categories to help you understand and imagine what we mean when we use the term "Christian resistance."

You can resist Christianly by taking a financial stand. Many people groups, including Christians, have used the power of a boycott to resist policies, systems, or companies that hurt and exploit. We mentioned coffee earlier in this book. Suppose you were to find out that your local neighborhood coffee shop purchased coffee from a supplier that did not pay their coffee bean producers fair market value for their product. What would you do? Could you go on supporting and investing in a company that was directly responsible for workers not being paid a livable wage? Would you be willing to take a stand and advocate for those workers whose lives are put in jeopardy by an unfair practice or policy? The companies that exploit coffee bean growers are addicted to your money. If you refuse to spend your money in their establishment, and if you spread the word and encourage others to buy their coffee elsewhere, you are practicing a financial form of resistance.

By the way, we can't plead ignorance. It's our responsibility to find these kinds of answers so that we don't unknowingly support systems that are damaging people and families. Living justice does not mean turning a blind eye on suffering or unfair practices around the world. The information is out there—living justice means being active—pursuing a response for what we know about and then learning more so that we can do more. The Bible echoes this idea, "Rescue those being led away to death; hold back those staggering toward slaughter. If you say, 'But we knew nothing about this,' does not he who weighs the heart perceive it? Does not he who guards your life know it? Will he not repay each person according to what he has done?" (Proverbs 24:11-12).

It is possible that your Christian resistance might take a political form. Again, it is important to understand the Christian obligation to be good citizens, obeying the laws of the land, so long as those laws are not in direct conflict with the character and nature of God. When there is this conflict, we must maintain our Christianity, resisting peacefully and responsibly.

Suppose your state were to enact legislation that would make it illegal for you to offer aid or comfort to anyone who might be labeled an undocumented citizen. (There are states that have already passed legislation like this—policies that criminalize the help you might want to give to a family in desperate need.) What would you do? What could you do?

It is not the purpose of this book to suggest political solutions to complex problems such as immigration. Governments (and involved Christians) need to carefully consider policies for difficult social problems such as this. Policies addressing difficult issues are one thing—policies making it illegal for Christians to do good to all people—that is something very different. At that point, Christians may need to pursue justice through resistance.

I have friends who are right now working toward changes in these sorts of laws. They have become frequent phone-callers and letter-writers, promising to support, with their votes, legislation and legislators with a greater good in mind, and promising to work against legislation and legislators who do not show compassion for those in difficult circumstances. Some of these same people are willing to challenge policies in court, hoping to have policies overturned that might be in conflict with other laws, policies, or legal decisions already on our law books. Perhaps you know attorneys who have made a career out of defending those who struggle to defend themselves. This kind of citizenship, this kind of resistance might be described as legal or political in nature.

The next form of resistance described here is much more personal, or even physical in nature. At times Christian resistors choose to lock arms with those in harm's way; they use their bodies to shield and protect and shelter those in need. No doubt you are aware of the horror of the holocaust in Germany, when Jews were rounded up and sentenced to die in concentration camps. If so, you may also be aware of the many stories of the resistance—stories that tell of one family hiding another, protecting them from the Nazi authorities.

Make no mistake, citizens in North America are not under the thumb of anything that even resembles a Nazi regime today. So does this kind of resistance still happen? And would it ever happen in one of our North American cities?

The answers are yes and yes. Here is one example.

There is a yacht club at Eastern College in Pennsylvania. But this isn't what it seems. Rather than a sailing boat "yacht," these students mean "Y.A.C.H.T." or Youth Against Complacency and Homelessness Today. Listen to them as they tell a story of Christian, non-violent resistance.

In September of 1995, a community of people, families and children, pitched tents in an open lot in the middle of North Philadelphia. The community was called Tent City, and the members were all a part of the Kensington Welfare Rights Union (KWRU), an organization created to help poor and homeless people of any age, race and religion unite and fight the current welfare and shelter systems. KWRU leaders and members are all welfare recipients who have been encouraged to stand up and make their voices heard to the system that has ignored them for so long. This was the first of several Tent Cities that they would continue to build throughout the following years.

A few students from Eastern College came across this small city late that Fall just as the KWRU members were looking to relocate because winter was closing in and they all needed a warmer place to sleep. The KWRU group discovered an abandoned Catholic church on 8th and York in North Philly, and proceeded to move into the filthy cathedral, lovingly referred to as "St. Ed's." They worked very hard to clean the place up, and were in need of a lot of things. The students became inspired by the determination that they saw in the nomadic group and decided to gather other students together to help out.

Shane Claiborne, Brooke Sexton, Josh Loveland, Scott Matney, Joe McCullough and others immediately began spreading awareness of this amazing and driven group of people in St. Ed's, and all of the needs that had to be met, from sorting clothing donations to babysitting and after-school tutoring for the children in the church. So many Eastern students answered their request for help that Brooke and Shane decided to organize their own branch of KWRU here at Eastern: the Y.A.C.H.T. club. Membership held no requirements except that all be willing to love and learn and fight against injustice.

When the city police threatened to forcefully remove the community from St. Ed's, Y.A.C.H.T. members stayed on call 24/7 if there ever was a need to rush in and protest their expulsion and alert the media. We got called in on an emergency a couple of times. We stayed all night and tried to get some sleep on the floor, staring up at the spacious cathedral ceiling, trying to forget (and remember?) our warm dorm beds, ready to face the cops at the doors in the morning. On one occasion, the Archdiocese of Philadelphia ordered the police to remove the homeless from "their" church. Eastern students, along with students from Penn, Temple, Drexel, Swarthmore and other colleges stayed the night to protest and, in the morning, had a rousing service. Finally, after a long fight, the city gave up.[29]

In fact, as the story goes, local firefighters, moved with compassion and inspired by these students, donated and installed equipment to bring the building up to fire code, again resisting the city's political efforts to remove this small community.

You don't have to look hard to find these sorts of examples of non-violent, Christian resistance. Dr. Martin Luther King and Rosa Parks exercised a very powerful, non-violent resistance that continues to shape our culture to this day. More recently, Nelson

Mandela and Bishop Desmond Tutu led the resistance that eventually defeated an entire political system, Apartheid, in South Africa. Even now, non-violent movements of resistance are taking place all over the world in places like the former Soviet Union.

But, more likely than not, you don't live in South Africa or the former Soviet Union. There may be some of you who will choose to go and live among those who are being treated unjustly and serve as non-violent resistors, locking arms with those in need, challenging the policies that do damage to people and the planet.

But the majority of us will remain here. Our efforts to resist, while they may take a lifetime to succeed, will rarely cause our deaths. When we take such a stand against violence, our lives will rarely be put in danger while we remain on this continent.

But that doesn't mean that some of us won't have very strong feelings about the violence taking place in other countries. You don't have to agree with the stance of pacifism—the utter rejection of violence as a tool for victory or change—but please don't do violence (physical or verbal) to those who might agree!

ONE LIFE OF SUBVERSIVE WORSHIP

Oscar Romero, the Catholic Archbishop in El Salvador in the late 1970s, embodied living as Jesus lived. Romero lived in very violent times in the midst of deep turmoil and civil war. Sociologists have shown that a central feature of this country was the concentration of wealth and power in the hands of a few at the expense of most people who were deeply impoverished. Historians have shown that the government used its military to support the persons who pulled the purse strings. Political scientists have shown that other countries helped to prop up this system for the benefit of their own companies' profits and regional power. The poor were not only excluded from any say over the political process, but most were forced to work in pitiful conditions with wages too low for most to survive on.

A catholic friend, Doug Harrison, once gave a brief Lenten reflection on the life of Archbishop Oscar Romero. We've included this reflection here as a witness to the possibility of a life lived with prophetic imagination. It is an example of how a life dedicated to worship was also a life dedicated to justice.

They elected Oscar Romero the Archbishop of El Salvador because they thought he would abstain from the political and economic struggles of the people of his diocese. They were right to assume that Bishop Romero had no political aspirations, unlike the rest of the Church, whose leaders had found security and profit from tending to the so called "spiritual lives" of people, as long as they ignored the profound oppression and suffering of the poor.

Romero only wanted to be Christian, to follow Jesus faithfully and fully. But what can it mean to be a shepherd of souls when your parishioners are being slaughtered and tortured by the thousands? What can it mean to be the bishop of a diocese whose churches are being commandeered as bunkers for the military as they slaughter your flock? How does one follow Jesus when the Body of Christ is being crucified again and again right in front of you?

For Romero, it did not mean running for election or taking up weapons. For Romero it meant learning how to celebrate the Eucharist in the right time and place. This priest, this follower of Jesus, re-occupied local parishes by simply walking in among the soldiers and initiating the service of the Lord's Supper.

The military stripped Romero naked in front of his congregation and other local townspeople for the purposes of public humiliation. He confronted the publicly executed illegal strip searches by learning to kneel down and pray. For who is more ashamed, the praying naked priest or the soldier who stripped him?

Romero learned how to be Christian. He learned to walk the way of the cross. In the last day of his life (March 23rd 1980) He preached these words "Without God, there can be no true concept of liberation. Temporary liberations yes; but definitive solid liberations—only people of faith reach them."

Later Romero continues by quoting Paul "Paul says of Christ 'to know him and the strength of his resurrection and the communion with his sufferings, dying with his same death that I may arrive one day at the resurrection of the dead."

The Bishop, who is unknowingly about to be shot, continues preaching: "Do you see how life recovers all of its meaning? And suffering then becomes a communion with Christ, the Christ that suffers, and death is a communion with the death that redeemed the world? Who can feel worthless before this treasure that one finds in Christ, that gives meaning to sickness, to pain, to oppression, to torture, to marginalization? . . . whoever believes in Christ knows that he is a victor and that the definitive victory will be that of truth and justice!"

What does the example of Bishop Romero call us to in the middle of this Lenten season, not unlike the one in which he died. He calls us to die, not for a cause, but for the one who gave His life for us. The death is no abstract spiritu-

al theology. It means we are to actually be reconciled to the poor in a country and culture that punishes those who go without. . . . It means we learn to pray in public at the right times and places with our bodies, with our lives.

Soon after Romero completed his sermon he began the consecration of the elements of the Lord's supper. As he lifted the cup an assassin took aim and drove a handful of bullets through his body. The blood of Christ poured out from the cup. The blood of Christ poured out from Romero's Chest.

Do we know You lord? We know You have loved us. But do we know You enough to follow You. Do we know enough of Your suffering to be with You in Your resurrection. Consecrate us now to Thy service Lord, By Thy power of grace divine. Let our souls look up with a steadfast hope and our will be lost in Thine. Draw us nearer precious Lord, to the cross where You died. Draw us nearer precious Lord to Thy precious bleeding side.[30]

The love for our brothers and sisters cannot be contained by borders as we witness to the God who "was reconciling the world to himself in Christ" (2 Corinthians 5:19). In God's reign, "There is neither Jew nor Greek, slave nor free, male nor female, for you are all one in Christ Jesus" (Galatians 3:28). The politics of Jesus stand in contrast to (and offers a salvation from) the politics of this age. Our faith calls for *koinonia*—a true community of worship that stands with our brothers and sisters around the globe, seeking God's best for them.

CHAPTER 5
IMAGINING A NEW COMMUNITY, A NEW HOPE

Why do we feed hungry people? Why should we even get involved? The issues of injustice are so large, so woven into our neighborhoods, cities, and world that, at times, it seems foolish to fight it. So why do we? We pursue justice for others because those facing injustice matter—and their lives should be protected and preserved.

If you and I are going to live out and embody justice, we are going to need the eyes of Jesus. We are going to need the ability to discern brokenness and exploitation, and at the same time strategy and hope. We are going to need the eyes of Christ to notice and weep for all who remain in harm's way.

In the mid-90s, there was a craze called Magic Eye, in which a three-dimensional image would "pop out" of a two-dimensional picture if you focused your eyes correctly. At first glance, the two-dimensional picture looked like a giant mess of garbled dots and nothingness. However, after learning how to focus on the image correctly, the pattern within the dots would appear.

There were those who claimed the whole thing was a hoax. No matter how long they stared at the picture, they were completely incapable of "seeing" the image. I used to be one of these people; then one day I finally saw something. Since that time, since I learned "how to see," I can actually find the image—it may take me awhile, but I eventually see it. Seeing the image is a matter of discernment—I have to discern the way the dots work together before I can see the hidden picture.

Similarly, so much of what we are called to do as Christians has to do with our ability to see and discern. We are called to see 1) God in the world, 2) ourselves as God sees us, 3) others as they are seen by God, and 4) the world (with its obstacles and opportunities) the same way God sees it. We try to do all of this while acknowledging that the world sometimes looks like nothing more than a giant mess of nothingness on a page.

Please don't misunderstand us, we are not saying we have it all figured out; there are plenty of days when life still looks like a mess to us, but, through practice and repetition, we are getting better at discerning God's vision. We are learning to see God, His pattern of behavior, and the promise and evidence of a new world where we didn't see it before. And as we do, we are developing and gaining a sense of godly wisdom.

The book of Proverbs contains some of the Bible's clearest statements on godly wisdom. These tidbits of knowledge were used to train young people in the hopes that they might develop the eyes of God. It says in Proverbs 15:17: "Better a meal of vegetables where there is love than a fattened calf with hatred." This proverb was written during a time where, like today, vegetables were typically less expensive than meat. So this proverb is saying that it is better to have less than the best *with* love instead of *the* best with hatred.

That's some pretty deep stuff. In fact, this proverb has been crucial in my (Jon) development as a husband, father, minister, and consumer. Slowly but surely God is granting me the wisdom to discern that the dominant culture is lying to me when it insists that I must have the best of everything. I'm being lied to when the culture tells me that my children really need more stuff. In truth, what my children really need is me and my presence. If that means we have to go without the best meat and eat vegetables, so be it. God is training me to see as He sees, and in the process, I am helping to train my children to see His way as well.[31]

I've noticed that my eyesight trains my attitudes and activities. As my eyesight improves, I realize more and more of my potential as a follower of Christ. All of us are no different in that respect. As you develop your Christian eyesight, you will be better able to discern the world around you. As you mature in your Christian understanding, your faithfulness and obedience to the vision of God will improve.

IMPROVING OUR VISION

Spiritual eyesight is not a given; blindness can, and does, occur. In fact, blindness is a constant theme throughout the Bible. Jesus accused the Pharisees of being blind to the Kingdom. We must diligently work to avoid spiritual blindness. One way we can do this is by asking ourselves this question, "Am I learning to see both the King and the Kingdom more clearly?"

Developing godly vision takes work, so we've included a list of things that we can do to develop our godly vision. All of these are exercises in discernment. We did them with a group from church; however, you could do them on your own. Our hope is that you will use your creativity to adapt these suggestions and that you will find new ways to strengthen your godly vision.

1. **Visit a different faith tradition and/or denomination's building.** Visit a Jewish Temple. Talk with Islamic friends. Go to eat at an Arabic restaurant. Take a tour of a Catholic cathedral. Visit other denominations different from your own—Baptist, Lutherans, Assemblies of God, Church of the Nazarene, Methodists,

Salvation Army. Go to a service or arrange to have someone give you a tour and share their distinctives. Ask questions and really get to know the similarities and differences you have with your religious neighbors.

Improved Eyesight will help you see and appreciate the similarities and differences you have with those of other denominations and faith traditions. It will help you see those of other faith traditions as people, and not as enemies.

2. **Watch and discuss a movie that deals with issues of justice.** Consider discussing films such as *The Mission, A Civil Action, Hotel Rwanda,* or *Les Misérables.* Some of these movies may deal with difficult subject matter, but it is fairly easy to find ones that do not glamorize tough topics (such as violence, racism, or human suffering).

Improved Eyesight helps us to see that the issues of violence, exploitation, prejudice, and hopelessness are present in our world today (and not just depicted in the movies).

3. **Visit the ethnic part of your town.** Eat the food. Talk to the people. Shop in the stores. Do whatever you can to immerse yourself in a different culture. Ask questions and try to gain an understanding for their way of life.

Improved Eyesight helps us to see that people are people, no matter what their skin color or cultural background.

4. **Visit with the chronically and terminally ill**. Go to an AIDS hospice. Spend time at a hospital ward for the chronically ill. Visit with the elderly, especially those in a nursing home who may not have family who can visit regularly. Spend enough time with the people there until it becomes comfortable for you. Come to the point where you are finally more aware of them and less aware of yourself.

Improved Eyesight helps us to see that we can be a form of grace in the lives of these Kingdom citizens who face death and loneliness.

5. **Go on a photo-shoot with your friends.** Make sure each person has a camera (digital preferably) and split up. Spend the first half of the time finding images and evidences of evil in the world. Spend the second half finding images that God is in fact present and active healing and recreating creation. When the time is up, go to someone's house and download all the pictures. Separate them into two folders—the "evil" pictures and the "God present" pictures. Then have someone put the images to music and watch your two slideshows. After watching the slideshows talk about what you saw. Ask people to explain the pictures they took, and in the process, learn from one another. Discuss how God would want us to be light in the midst of darkness.

Improved Eyesight helps us see that which we normally don't see. It opens our eyes to the everyday realities that we normally block out.

Developing godly vision still seems different and foreign to me. I still find myself fighting the constraints of a consumer culture that has reached all the way inside the church. So when you find yourself struggling against the consumerism, don't become discouraged. Re-training your eyesight is difficult and the "buy now (whether we need it or not)" habits you've grown up with are difficult to break. However, keep persevering because godly eyesight and discernment are necessary ingredients in having a prophetic imagination.

THE PROPHETIC IMAGINATION REVISITED

Remember what we said earlier about the role of prophets and the prophetic imagination? One of the roles of the prophet was taking a critical look at the culture around them. They were a voice speaking about wrong that everyone else seemed to just accept. They were the hands and feet that took action to see that good was being done for those who couldn't do it for themselves.

In his wonderful book *Life on the Vine: Cultivating the Fruit of the Spirit*, Philip Kenneson uses the analogy of growing plants to communicate what it means to grow the life of the Spirit in us. The same type of language helps us understand how we develop the prophetic imagination. It is something that must be cultivated. We must break up the soil of our hearts that has been hardened. We must plant seeds of understanding. To grow our prophetic imagination, we must water our lives with the love of God that moves us to action. Kenneson explains it this way:

> Cultivating love in the midst of market-style exchanges,
> Cultivating joy in the midst of manufactured desire,
> Cultivating peace in the midst of fragmentation,
> Cultivating patience in the midst of productivity,
> Cultivating kindness in the midst of self-sufficiency,
> Cultivating goodness in the midst of self-help,
> Cultivating faithfulness in the midst of impermanence,
> Cultivating gentleness in the midst of aggression,
> Cultivating self-control in the midst of addiction.[32]

Here is one example of how we cultivated the prophetic imagination in our (Jon's) church. Our church is in the more affluent, mostly Caucasian part of town. Recently we decided to sponsor a city-wide discussion on racism and the Church's response and responsibilities. It was a difficult topic, but together we felt we were being led by the Spirit to address the issue in our community. We began to *imagine* how our community might be different if we let God help us work through a difficult issue like this one. Soon our imagination began to take action.

We decided to talk about racism with those different from us. We invited Dr. Reed, the pastor of a vibrant African-American congregation; Jorge, a leader in the Hispanic community; and Shirley, an immigrant to the United States who is now an attorney employed by the Catholic Church to advocate for immigrants. In preparation for this event, several members of our ministry staff met with Pastor Reed and his staff. We were insistent that our conversation about racism (which we called the Forum) would not be mere words thrown at a problem.

The Forum took place in early 2006. Since then we've shared many services together. We've sung together. We've served one another the bread and cup of the Eucharist. We've eaten together in the hopes of birthing a new reality. Friendships now exist where they didn't or couldn't before. As my children watch and participate, we're recreating a world in which lines can be erased, and God's dream for life can be lived more fully and completely. Many of us can't help but think that things are being put right.

The prophets can teach us a lot about justice. Remember, for the Old Testament prophets, justice described how the people were to live in the world in relation to each other (this meant relating justly to those within their group, and to those outside of it). The people of God were to practice justice by showing grace and mercy toward those who had no power to secure it for themselves. They were to protect and defend those who were helpless and powerless. They were to identify with those pushed to the margins of society. They were to wrap their story up with those who suffered. Likewise, we, as the people of God today, are to continue living in that model of living justice.

In her book *The Cloister Walk*, Kathleen Norris notes that "a prophet's task is to reveal the fault lines hidden beneath the comfortable surface of the worlds we invent for ourselves, the national myths as well as the little lies and delusions of control and security that get us through the day."[33]

A prophetic voice will not gloss over injustice or oppression; it will not be silent in the face of bigotry, racism, sexism, or false pride. The prophetic voice is energized by the same God who brought Israel out of slavery and oppression. Prophets stand as a counter voice to those who would allow the allure of power, ambition, and self-serving self-righteousness to blind them to the things of God. A prophetic voice sweeps away all the trappings of religion and answers the question, "What does God ask of me?" with the reply, "To simply do justice, love mercy, and walk humbly with my God" (Micah 6:8, author's paraphrase).

WE ARE HOW WE WORSHIP

Liturgies (the form, order, and pattern of worship) are crucially important because it is in worship that we nurture our imagination. If we are just waiting for the end to come, then that influences how we worship—and how we view the world. If we just want to worship until we "can be taken out this mess," then we will sing, pray, read Scripture, and perhaps even serve with that end in mind. The imagination we nurture will be more about self-preservation than it will be about the preservation and restoration of all people and all creation.

But if we see worship as the rehearsal of the hope that God has for the church to overcome the worst in the world, then we will have an "others" view rather than a "self-preservation" view. We will recognize that in overcoming the world through the death and resurrection of Christ, God has unleashed the beginning of the end. Our worship and liturgy will then nurture our prophetic imagination. We will recognize that:

- We give our gifts of time and money in the hope that the redistribution of resources will protect the lives of those in harm's way.
- We sing in the hope that we will again realize this is "our Father's world."
- We pray the Lord's Prayer in the hope that we will some-day both believe it and embody it.
- We read and listen to the Word so we can be instruments of justice and redemption, partnering with God to usher in the new Kingdom that is now and not yet finished.
- We partake of the Eucharist to remember the love that makes life possible.
- We are baptized in celebration of our new self-definition and citizenship.
- We serve to put flesh on the gospel.

THE PROPHETIC IMAGINATION IN USE

What would a Church that uses its prophetic imagination look like? Imagine a church that reflects upon the central question: What does it mean to be the Body of Christ in the world?

Imagine a church that sees its mission to develop a catechism ("a book giving a brief summary of the basic principles of Christianity in question-and-answer form")[34] that will not only help us learn how we are to be in the world but will also provide credible alternatives to the ways of the world that prevent us from being one in body and spirit (Ephesians 4:4). Imagine if all our churches were mini-monasteries[35] or seminaries training the Body to study scripture and Christian history in order to discern how we may "do justice and love mercy." Imagine if our universities became resources to help facilitate such profound nurturing of the prophetic imagination.

Imagine a church that marks time by the Christian calendar rather than the rhythms of any particular homeland, industry, or ethnic preference. Celebrating Advent as opposed to the "Christmas shopping season" would help us to reform our consumer spending addictions. Disciplining ourselves for the 40 days of Lent would help us slow down and listen more carefully to the cries of those who regularly go without.

Imagine a Church that spends the time and energy needed to develop disciplined disciples who practice love and unity, who listen to and hear one another, and who acknowledge the profound gifts God has granted to everyone. Imagine mission trips that raise enough money to not only go on the trip but to also provide all the necessary materials and wages for local contractors. These mission teams would not do any of the work once they arrived at their destination; they would allow the local contractors to build (thus, providing them with jobs). Instead, the team members would spend time in the local people's homes sharing stories of life and faith—being with them, loving them, listening to them, and learning from them.

Imagine a North American church that would use its resources to sponsor a mission trip team from a church in a country without easy access to travel or resources. Such trips would generate understanding about discerning God's economy and just how much is enough.[36] Imagine a church that could imagine itself developing sister-church relations with a church in another part of the world that may be struggling for resources. The church members in both congregations would broaden their horizons; they would begin to care for one another in all facets of life; they would listen to each other, pray together, learn about one another's cultural worlds, and redistribute resources as each had need.

Imagine a Church marked by generosity and reciprocity where the people of God work together and direct resources until all who are able can find meaningful and productive work that pays a livable wage. Image a Church where disciples are "of one heart and soul" and where everything is "held in common" so that there is "not a needy person among them" (Acts 4:32, 34).[37]

Imagine a Church that identifies with, suffers alongside, and uses its resources to help the outcasts of society. Imagine a Church that needs no compassionate ministries structure or arm because the entire Body of Christ is engaged in and working toward providing the hungry something to eat, the thirsty something to drink, the stranger a place to stay, the naked with clothes to wear, providing the sick comfort and care, and visiting those in prison. Imagine a Church whose life exudes peace, justice, love, and grace for the "least of these."

The Body of Christ is both the messenger and the message. We are a peculiar people of love and thanksgiving who are ambassadors of reconciliation in a broken and fallen world. We bear witness to the reign of God in word and deed. We are called to be a holy people with discipleship practices that invite us into the life of holiness.

CONCLUDING THOUGHTS

There will be some pain involved in becoming a person of justice and righteousness. You will be asked to become aware of the world in ways you haven't yet. You will be asked to sacrifice in support of causes and peoples. You will, in all probability, have to adjust or even replace your definitions of important words like poor, rich, enough, abundance, freedom, and power. This process may take a long time, so stay with it.

To help you on this journey and process, here are some steps and ideas to give you a place to start:

- **Practice and develop great audacity.** With great boldness, confront unfairness, inequality, and instances where justice is absent. Don't just look out there in far-off world areas where war and poverty make news; you *must* include these issues, but be sure to include subjects and issues that are close to home, within arm's reach.

- **Learn to work backwards.** Paint the end picture of the dream of God for all of creation (for an idea of this, examine Isaiah 11, the kingdom of Peace). Justice seeks to accomplish the reality of this kingdom of Peace. As you take action, make sure that your actions are always in line with the hopes and dreams of God. If you want to take up the cause of the poor in your neighborhood, you can't rob the banks and shoot the guards in the process. Those actions do not move creation toward the kingdom of Peace.

- **Become the ultimate team player.** Recognize quickly that while you can take individual action, you must partner with others to make the greatest impact and not lose heart yourself. Look around; there might already be an organization out there, even close to you, that is dreaming your same dream for your cause. If not, do the best you can to facilitate, organize, and equip others around you to serve. Remember, God has made a practice of calling the young to speak to a broken and power-hungry world. But you don't get to use your youth to be disorganized, lazy, or stupid. Harness the energy around you so that people are working together, in harmony, not in competition.

- **Let the sky be the limit.** The world faces enormous challenges. The factors in question may seem too huge for you to do anything about, but don't get intimidated so that you do nothing. Do something; chip away and know that the God who called the prophets and stood by them, will stand by you as well.

As we've reached the end of this journey together, we'd like to leave you with this prayer: "Heavenly Father, in your Word you have given us a vision of that holy City to which the nations of the world bring their glory: Behold and visit, we pray, the cities of the earth. Renew the ties of mutual regard which form our civic life. Send us honest and able leaders. Enable us to eliminate poverty, prejudice, and oppression, that peace may prevail with righteousness, and justice with order, and that men and women from different cultures and with differing talents may find with one another the fulfillment of their humanity; through Jesus Christ our Lord. Amen." [38]

NOTES

1. Brueggemann, Walter. *A Commentary on Jeremiah: Exile and Homecoming* (Grand Rapids: Eerdmans, 1998), 79.

2. See Genesis 1:27-28; 2:15, 19-20. In these verses, we see God giving humankind responsibility for the earth.

3. Wright, NT. *Simply Christian* (San Francisco: Harper, 2006), 13.

4. <http://www.pbs.org/kcts/affluenza/>. Accessed April 12, 2007; also a book—*Affluenza: The All-Consuming Epidemic* by John De Graaf, David Wann, and Thomas H. Naylor (San Francisco: Berrett-Koehler Publishers, 2002). The word combines "affluent" (wealthy) with "influenza" (the cold virus we call the "flu"). The idea is that the desire for wealth has spread among us rapidly like a contagious sickness.

5. The sociologist Max Weber argued that affluence, i.e. the accumulation of wealth (capital), was in part a product of Protestant Christian beliefs and practices, what he called the "Protestant Ethic." This comes from his book, *The Protestant Ethic and the Spirit of Capitalism* (New York: Penguin Books, 2002).

6. Robbins, Richard H. *Global Problems and the Culture of Capitalism* (Boston: Allyn and Bacon, 2002), 14.

7. Leach, William. *Land of Desire: Merchants, Power, and the Rise of a New American Culture* (New York: Pantheon, 1993).

8. "How Much Debt Can We Afford?" The Des Moines Business Record, Dec. 4, 2005, <http://www.businessrecord.com/Main.asp?SectionID=40&SubSectionID=75&ArticleID=2355>. Accessed May 29, 2007.

9. Nikki Finke, "Dumb and Dumberer," LA Weekly, May 29, 2003, <http://www.laweekly.com/general/deadline-hollywood/dumb-and-dumberer/9923/?page=1>. Accessed May 29, 2007. Other major media conglomerates include Vivendi/Universal, Sony/BME, and EMI.

10. McChesney, Robert, W. *Rich Media, Poor Democracy: Communication Politics in Dubious Times* (New York, NY: New Press, 2000).

11. Krista Ramsey, "Are our children overindulged?" cincinnati.com: The Enquirer, Sept. 25, 2005, <http://news.cincinnati.com/apps/pbcs.dll/article?AID=/20050925/EDIT03/509250307/-1/CINCI>. Accessed May 29, 2007.

12. economics. Dictionary.com. *Dictionary.com Unabridged (v 1.1)*. Random House, Inc. <http://dictionary.reference.com/browse/economics>. Accessed April 27, 2007.

13. God may or may not be calling your family to give your house back to those who owned it before you. Did your family take advantage of those previous owners? Were they in circumstances where they had to sell, and now they cannot provide for themselves? If so, then you might want to talk about giving their house back! If this is not the case, then you are probably living by this principle—at least as far as home ownership is concerned. Those of us who live in this global economy where so many things are connected must ask ourselves this question: "Are there ways that I am tak-

ing advantage of someone else halfway around the world by my lifestyle and the economic systems in which I participate?"

14. A phrase coined by Donald Kraybill, *The Upside-Down Kingdom* (Scottsdale, PA: Herald Press, 1978).

15. Cobb, John B. 2000. "Consumerism, Economism and the Christian Faith." Lecture delivered at the Buddhist-Christian meeting in Tacoma, Washington, August 2000. <http://www.religion-online.org/showarticle.asp?title=1089>. Accessed March 30, 2007.

16. Kavanaugh, John. *Following Christ in a Consumer Society* (Maryknoll, NY: Orbis, 1991), 34.

17. As John Cobb put it, "As the general standard of living rises among those with whom we associate, our notion of a 'modest' level of consumption rises." Cobb, John B. "Consumerism, Economism and the Christian Faith." Lecture delivered at the Buddhist-Christian meeting in Tacoma, Washington, August 2000. <http://www.religion-online.or/showarticle.asp?title=1089>. Accessed March 30, 2007.

18. Adapted from Wesley, John. 1788. "On Riches" (Sermon 108). <http://wesley.nnu.edu/john_wesley/sermons/108.htm>. Accessed March 30, 2007.

19. Adapted from Wesley, John. 1744. "The Use of Money" (Sermon 50). <http://wesley.nnu.edu/john_wesley/sermons/050.htm>. Accessed March 30, 2007.

20. Adapted from Wesley, John. 1744. "On Riches" (Sermon 108). <http://wesley.nnu.edu/john_wesley/sermons/108.htm>. Accessed March 30, 2007.

21. obsolescence. Dictionary.com. *Dictionary.com Unabridged (v 1.1)*. Random House, Inc. <http://dictionary.reference.com/browse/obsolescence>. Accessed April 13, 2007.

22. See Phillip Kenneson's poignant social analysis of the challenges of modernity to our ability to cultivate the Fruit of the Spirit in Christian community: *Life on the Vine: Cultivating the Fruit of the Spirit in Christian Community* (Downer's Grove, IL: InterVarsity Press, 1999).

23. Stone, Brian. *Evangelism after Christendom: The Theology and Practice of Christian Witness* (Grand Rapids: Brazos Press, 2007), 178.

24. See Walter Brueggemann's *The Prophetic Imagination* (Minneapolis: Augsburg Fortress Publishing, 1978).

25. subversive. Dictionary.com. *WordNet® 3.0*. Princeton University. <http://dictionary.reference.com/browse/subversive>. Accessed May 02, 2007.

26. Brueggemann, Walter. *Deep Memory, Exuberant Hope: Contested Truth in a Post-Christian World* (Minneapolis: Augsburg Fortress Publishers, 2000).

27. Claiborne, Shane. *The Irresistible Revolution: Living as an Ordinary Radical* (Grand Rapids: Zondervan, 2006).

28. Brueggemann, Walter. *Deep Memory, Exuberant Hope: Contested Truth in a Post-Christian World* (Minneapolis: Augsburg Fortress Publishers, 2000).

29. "Y.A.C.H.T.'s History," from <http://www.eastern.edu/campus/groups/yacht/history.html>. Accessed on May 7, 2007.

30. Lenten Address by Doug Harrison at Point Loma Nazarene University in the Spring of 2002. Manuscript given to the author.

31. Brueggeman, Walter. *Texts Under Negotiation* (Minneapolis: Fortress Press, 1993), 87-89.

32. Kenneson, Phillip D. *Life on the Vine: Cultivating the Fruit of the spirit in Christian Community,* (Downers Grove, IL: InterVarsity Press, 1999), 7.

33. Norris, Kathleen. *The Cloister Walk* (New York: Riverhead Trade, 1997).

34. catechism. Dictionary.com. *The American Heritage® Dictionary of the English Language, Fourth Edition.* Houghton Mifflin Company, 2004. <http://dictionary.reference.com/browse/catechism>. Accessed April 17, 2007.

35. Consider this challenging thought on this idea of being mini-monasteries: "The restoration of the church will surely come only from a new type of monasticism which has nothing in common with the old but a complete lack of compromise in a life lived in accordance with the Sermon on the Mount in the discipleship of Christ. I think it is time to gather people together to do this. . . ." Extract of a letter written by Dietrich Bonhoeffer to his brother Karl-Friedrick on the 14th of January, 1935. (Source: John Skinner, Northumbria Community).

36. See Ross and Gloria Kinsler's *The Biblical Jubilee and the Struggle for Life: An Invitation to Personal, Ecclesial and Social Transformation* (Maryknoll, NY: Orbis Books, 1999). See also *God's Economy: Biblical Studies from Latin America* (Maryknoll, NY: Orbis Books, 2005).

37. For an excellent essay on giving voice to poor people and advocating for their equal participation in work and in theological reflection, see Steve de Gruchy's "Of Agency, Assets and Appreciation: Seeking some Commonalities between Theology and Development,"*Journal of Theology for Southern Africa*, Nov. 2003, p. 20-39.

38. "A Prayer for Cities" *Book of Common Prayer*, 1979 Edition.